ET TU, BRUTE?

ET TU, BRUTE?

THE MURDER OF CAESAR AND

POLITICAL ASSASSINATION

GREG WOOLF

Harvard University Press
Cambridge, Massachusetts
2007

Printed in the United States of America

First published in the United Kingdom by
Profile Books Ltd,
3A Exmouth House
Pine Street
Exmouth Market
London EC1R OJH

Library of Congress Cataloging-in-Publication Data

Woolf, Greg.
Et tu, Brute?: a short history of political murder / Greg Woolf.
p. cm.
Originally published: London: Profile Books, 2006.
Includes index.
ISBN-13: 978-0-674-02684-1 (alk. paper)
ISBN-10: 0-674-02684-5 (alk. paper)
1. Caesar, Julius—Assassination. 2. Assassination-History. I. Title.
DG267. W66 2007
937. 05–dc22
2007009150

For Jo

CONTENTS

PREFACE

Jean-Léon Gérôme's great canvas says it all. The sombre majesty of a marbled senate house, figured like a cathedral hung with trophies. In the middle, standing in a pool of light, a group of senators in snowy togas wave their daggers triumphantly in the air. Beside them the statue of Victory seems to stretch out her arm in solidarity. In the background we glimpse other senators running out into the dazzling heat of a Roman afternoon. Frightened? Excited? There are just a few signs of a scuffle, a few wooden chairs knocked over, an abandoned cloak, perhaps a little blood that will be easily wiped up off the mosaic floor. Except, that is, for the bottom left-hand corner, where a crumbled heap of white turns out to be the body of the victim, a smudge of red on its chest, one arm outstretched, its head entirely covered. Great Caesar. Above him, barely visible in the gloom, looms the massive nude statue of his sometime ally and eventual bitter enemy, Pompey. The scene seems curiously silent. The conspirators should be shouting Liberty! There should be panic and mayhem. But the actors are already moving off-stage, leaving the monument and the corpse alone together in a vast columned space that disappears into the gloom ... like ancient Rome itself.

It was William Shakespeare who gave Julius Caesar the

1. The conspirators flee the scene of Caesar's murder in Jean-Léon Gérôme's
Death of Caesar. *At first glance we hardly notice the dictator's corpse,*
crumpled in the bottom left hand corner.

line 'Et tu Brute?' If Caesar did say something of the kind, it was in Greek, and he reproached Brutus not by name but as 'my son'. Yet Shakespeare's Caesar had to speak to a Renaissance audience that like the bard himself had 'small Latin and less Greek', and Brutus had to be, at least potentially, a Brute for murdering his friend and benefactor. Brutus is not wholly a Brute for Shakespeare, any more than Caesar is certainly a tyrant. Others disagreed violently. For Dante, Brutus's crime had been second only to that of Judas. For Ben Jonson, writing his *Sejanus* less than five years after Shakespeare's play was first performed, Brutus was

> the constant Brutus, that (being proof
> Against all charm of benefits) did strike
> So brave a blow into the monster's heart
> That sought unkindly to captive his country.

And we continue to disagree. Caesar and his murderers have each been admired and vilified down the centuries. That is one reason why Shakespeare's *Julius Caesar*, a play about a murdered tyrant who did not behave like a tyrant, and an assassin who loves and honours his victim, continues in almost constant performance. Since the Renaissance the murder of Caesar has provided a stock figure for talking about tyrannicide. Playwrights and essayists in most European languages have used it to ask: When might the murder of a political leader be justified? Theologians and philosophers have returned to it to ask whether a tyrant's subjects have a right or even a duty to murder him. Even today, the story raises uncomfortable questions. We too, or at least our leaders, are tempted to unsheathe our daggers to end tyranny and bring about a bloody birth of liberty. But does it work? And what kind of liberty do we recover when it derives from a crime? Finally Brutus's dilemma – my friend or my country? – is a perennial one.

The murder of the Roman general Julius Caesar on 15 March 44 BC – the Ides of March of the consulship of Julius Caesar and Mark Antony, as the Roman calendar had it – lies at the midpoint of Roman history. It is at once the last act of the long fall of the Roman republic, and the bloody beginning of the Roman empire. The republic did not only die in Caesar. His death was one of a cluster of savage blows. Cato, a stern and irascible Stoic philosopher who had never compromised in condemning criminality and opposing tyranny, committed suicide towards the end of the civil war, just as others were reconciling themselves with the dictator. His death sent shudders of horror and guilty admiration through Rome, and enraged Caesar. Then there was Cicero, another orator and another moralist, but as different from Cato as it is possible to imagine. Cato had a famous name and feared nothing. Cicero was no nobleman and had no family reputation, and was desperately concerned about how others viewed him. But he was also urbane and sophisticated in so far as his purse allowed him to be, and his career had depended on his wit and skill at brokering alliances. Reconciled unhappily to dictatorship, he came out of scholarly retirement after Caesar's death to oppose the savage rise to power of Caesar's right-hand man, Mark Antony. For his pains he was hunted down and murdered, his head and hands cut off and displayed on the orators' platform in the Roman forum. Finally there were the conspirators themselves. One Roman historian called Cassius 'the last of the Romans'. And there was Brutus, 'the noblest Roman of them all'. So many blows to kill the Roman republic.

Cato, Caesar, Cicero, Brutus and Cassius will each play their part in this story. Together their deaths mark the failure of a political culture, the end of ancient republicanism. The survivors of the bloodbath, Mark Antony and Caesar's great nephew Octavian, slugged it out for another decade and a half for control of Rome. Only after the great naval victory at Actium of 31 BC – and the suicides of Antony and Cleopatra that followed – was the field finally clear for Octavian to found a Roman monarchy far more autocratic than the dictatorship to which Brutus and Cassius, Cato and Cicero had so bitterly objected. More impressive yet, Octavian somehow managed to avoid Julius Caesar's fate. The same could not be said for many of his successors. Yet somehow the Roman empire survived assassinations better than the republic had. There were few civil wars after the death of Antony, and 'the glorious majesty of the Roman peace' was rarely disturbed.

Caesar's murder is more or less the midpoint chronologically of a millennium and a half of Roman history. The city was believed to have been founded in 753 BC, although archaeology can in fact trace settlement on the Seven Hills from rather earlier. Seven hundred years after Caesar's death, the empire had lost, partially regained and then definitively abandoned all the lands west of the Adriatic to a mass of Germanic peoples. As the Islamic conquests poured out of Arabia, Rome lost most of the lands south and east of the Mediterranean too. The Byzantine empire that continued Rome's name into the eighth century AD and beyond was a purely Balkan and Anatolian power. Yet Caesar's name and story survived, in the libraries of Constantinople and in the monasteries of the west, waiting to be reawakened during the Renaissance.

None of the principal actors could have predicted the significance of the Ides of March. But they might have agreed how Rome had reached the crisis. For a hundred years the city had been undisputed mistress of the Mediterranean world. It had survived Hannibal and destroyed his city of Carthage. Of the kingdoms set up on the ruins of the Persian empire by Alexander the Great's generals, only one – Cleopatra's Egypt – had not been humiliated by Roman arms or diplomacy. Their wealth had poured into Rome, enriching the generals, the city and eventually most of the nobility. Cicero and his generation lived in houses the splendour of which would have amazed their fathers. Marble was brought from overseas to construct first great temples and then grand houses for the wealthy. They enjoyed the paid services of the greatest Greek intellectuals of the day. They owned great rural retreats in the Alban and Sabine hills, and some had pleasure villas on the Bay of Naples. These were adorned with artworks – bronzes, marble statues, paintings

2. *Julius Caesar at his most sinister, as a black onyx bust from Egypt.*

and libraries plundered from Greek temples and palaces and purchased from ancient cities, spectacular statue groups made to order by the best sculptors in the world, working in Rome in the best materials Roman money could buy. The nobles of Rome, along with talented newcomers like Cicero, were the rulers of the world, the equals of kings. Meanwhile Rome's armies marched ever further afield, to Atlantic Spain, to the Channel, to the Caspian and across the Syrian desert, and prowled along the margins of the Sahara, returning with gold, silver and slaves.

Yet, in grim counterpoint to her conquest of the world, Rome was tearing herself apart. The proceeds of empire were shared unevenly. This led to fierce rivalry among the aristocracy and simmering resentment among the Roman poor who doubled as her soldiery. By the time of Julius Caesar's birth, in 100 BC, some Roman politicians had already begun to seek power by championing the discontented masses. At first, they wanted subsidised or free grain and a share of public land. Soon they wanted a say in every area of policy, sovereignty in a word. Typically the leaders of the popular party came from the most elevated families: men like Caesar in other words, rather than *arrivistes* like Cicero. Caesar was a patrician, descended from a family so old that it claimed descent from the goddess Venus herself. His aunt had married the popular hero Marius, a brilliant general who made his name finishing off a long African war that had been bungled by his aristocratic predecessors at the cost of many Roman lives. Marius then went on to save Italy from German invasions from north of the Alps. He also for the first time ever recruited an army from the mass of Romans who had absolutely no land of their own, soldiers of fortune who depended on him utterly: they would follow him not only to the ends of the earth but even into the streets of its capital.

In the event, it was not Marius who marched on Rome but his rival Sulla. Aristocratic and arrogant, his politics were the opposite of Marius's and he had far less scruple. When in 88 BC he was deprived by popular politicians of a lucrative foreign command, he refused to stand down and marched his troops into the city. He installed his senatorial friends and set off for his eastern war. When he returned, seven years later, he made himself dictator and began slaughtering his enemies. Caesar was one of those who had to flee for his life. The experience of Sulla's dictatorship never left him. The office of dictator had originally been an emergency command, used for example in the darkest days of the Hannibalic War, when debate and consultation could have been fatal. Sulla showed Caesar how the dictatorship might be an instrument for remaking Rome in his image. He also taught him the grim consequences of retribution. For Sulla brought Rome no lasting peace. He resigned his dictatorship and died soon after, and the civil strife – the root causes of which he had never addressed – at once reappeared. The powerful rival generals of the next generation were his lieutenants, Crassus and Pompey. Within a decade, they had dismantled their master's constitution and set off on brilliant careers of their own.

Crassus courted the popular party. Good at speaking and very rich, he was surrounded by more desperate and more committed men than himself. Young Caesar, noble but poor, was among them. Cicero might have been: he had begun his career riding the anti-Sullan bandwagon, but he was temperamentally no revolutionary and cared too much for the respect of other senators. Pompey, in the meantime, seemed indifferent to anything but his own military success. While revolution simmered in Rome throughout the sixties, Pompey was away flushing the Mediterranean of pirates, conquering the kings of Asia, taking Roman arms further than they had ever been before. All Rome was in his shadow, and a large part adored him. As Shakespeare put it,

> Knew you not Pompey? Many a time and oft
> Have you climbed up to walls and battlements,
> To towers and windows, yea, to chimney-tops,
> Your infants in your arms, and there have sat
> The livelong day, with patient expectation,
> To see great Pompey pass the streets of Rome.

3. This bust of Pompey, found in a tomb just outside Rome, illustrates how the great general hoped to be seen. The face is probably a good likeness, and not in the least idealised, but the crop of hair curling over his head alludes to portraits of Alexander that were already well known. A world-conqueror, then, but a Roman one.

But the nobility, remembering Sulla, feared his return. Meanwhile Caesar clambered up the conventional career ladder, elected young to prestigious priesthoods thanks to his patrician blood, winning the unglamorous junior offices of first, quaestor, and then praetor while Pompey dazzled Rome. Around this time, the story goes, Caesar wept to see a statue of Alexander the Great, reflecting how little he himself had achieved by the age at which Alexander had conquered the world. The tears maybe had a topical bitterness. Pompey too was now the Great, and he now named cities after himself just as Alexander had done. On his portraits his hair mimicked Alexander's and the Greeks treated him with honours they usually reserved for gods. Caesar renewed his efforts. Spectacular bribery (with borrowed money) won him the senior priesthood in Rome. Brilliant oratory made him one of the rising stars of the popular party. But he narrowly escaped being incriminated in a conspiracy suppressed by Cicero which cost some of his allies their lives.

Pompey's return changed everything. Spurned by the senate, he made common cause with Crassus and Caesar and together the three of them dominated Roman politics for a decade. Crassus's wealth and Pompey's loyal veterans enabled them to take what they wanted from the state. One thing that both Caesar and Crassus wanted was great military commands. Crassus's command against the Parthian empire ended in humiliation and death, but Caesar enjoyed ten years of spectacular campaigning from the south of France to Britain and the Rhineland. He returned debt-free, indeed rich, with an army prepared to follow him against Rome and Pompey himself. Cicero, Cato and their allies had worked hard to drive a wedge between the two men. But their success in doing so had the opposite effects to those they desired. Faced with the order to dismiss his armies and return to Rome a private citizen, Caesar chose instead to lead his army across the river Rubicon, which divided his province from Italy. Sweeping down the peninsula he faced little opposition and soon Pompey, with his senatorial supporters, fled across the Adriatic to what is now northern Greece. Caesar followed, and at the battle of Pharsalus in 48 BC, Pompey was defeated. Many of his supporters, Cicero, Brutus and Cassius among them, threw themselves on Caesar's mercy. Pompey fled to Egypt, where he was murdered, and Caesar spent much of his short dictatorship hunting down Pompeian armies around the Mediterranean. But he also had a clear programme for Rome. He would be a dictator like Sulla, but one who stood for the people, not the senate, and there would be no murders and no exiles, nor would he resign and see his work undone as Sulla had done. Energetic projects absorbed Caesar in the autumn of 45 and the spring of 44: there were public works to build, the calendar to reform, legislation and administrative reform needed. He was also preparing a great campaign to avenge Crassus (and surpass Pompey) in the east. His army was due to leave in late March. Rumours spread that before he left he sought the title of king. It would be difficult to touch him once he was in the field, let alone after a triumphal return. Time was running out for the opposition. With something like desperation, and no clear idea of what to do if they succeeded, they planned to face Caesar in the senate meeting scheduled for the Ides of March, and win back liberty for Rome.

It has been said that we know more about the events of the Ides of March than of any other day in Roman history. Certainly ancient writers tell us an immense amount about it. But conspiracy to murder is a messy business and all was confusion within seconds of Casca's first blow. Much is still unclear, but in the first chapter we watch the ripples of fear and rumour spreading out like the blood from all those wounds. Julius Caesar's murder had deep roots: Chapter 2 surveys these. It is perhaps the first occasion in history when we can hear contemporaries and participants rehearsing arguments for regicide that would become all too familiar from the seventeenth century on. After Caesar, killing a failing emperor became almost a routine and almost never led to civil strife. The third chapter asks why so many emperors died violently, and how Rome learned to shrug its shoulders and carry on. And what of the aftershocks of Caesar's death? The last chapter follows the history of Cato, Caesar and the rest into the modern day. Idealised, schematised and reduced into vivid symbols, the main protagonists were passed like batons in a relay race by first Greek and Latin and then vernacular classics up to the present day, where admirable, tyrannical, pitiable and ambitious Caesar faces an uncertain future.

1

'THEN FALL, CAESAR!'

The most spectacular building in all of Republican Rome was the theatre of Pompey. Larger than any theatre built before or since, it towered over the Field of Mars, the low floodplain half encircled by a bend in the river Tiber. It took half a decade to construct, and was finally inaugurated, in 55 BC, just over a decade before Caesar's murder. It was built entirely in marble, and at the summit of a great curve of seats that could hold 40,000 spectators stood a temple to Victorious Venus. The seats themselves were divided into seats for senators and foreign ambassadors, seats for the knights, seats for commoners, so that all the elaborate hierarchies of Roman society were displayed each in their place. Behind the stage stood a forest of columns, and behind that a great park, enclosed by a portico nearly 180 metres long and 135 metres wide. Plane trees offered shade in the fierce Roman summer. The poet Propertius would write of its gurgling fountains – it was the sound of water, not extravagant jets, that entranced Romans – and golden drapes. Propertius and his fellow poet Ovid found in the garden a suitable setting for lovers' meetings. It was a Roman pleasure dome, one that brought into the heart of the city and made available to the people a style of luxury that had until then been confined to the private gardens of the aristocracy's rural retreats.

4. The ground plan of Pompey's great theatre is still visible in this aerial view of the Campo Marzio in Rome. The building itself is long gone but a few traces can be seen in basement bistros, and the curve of the cavea is clear in the line of the via Grotta Pinta.

In the surrounding cloisters were displayed paintings and statues, most of them plundered from the eastern provinces Pompey had conquered. Pliny the elder, writing a century later, listed the Greek masterpieces still on display in the portico. Some portrayed characters and scenes from Greek myth: Cadmus and Europa painted by Antiphilos, a tableau by Pausias depicting a great sacrifice of cattle, a noted *trompe l'oeil* by Polygnotos. There were statues of famous courtesans, statues of women from Greek myth who had given birth to strange monsters – minotaurs and elephants among them. And there were fourteen statues made by the sculptor Coponius that depicted ethnic groups, commemorating their conquest by Pompey, the Roman Alexander, Rome's greatest general, who with his allies Crassus and Caesar had enslaved the Roman state for half a decade when the theatre was dedicated.

Behind the garden, at the other end of the great complex from the theatre proper, were a series of great chambers. One of them, the curia, provided for meetings of the Roman senate. The senate was the ancient aristocratic council of the city, composed only of the rich, mostly of former magistrates, entirely of men. Many of its members regarded it as the legitimate government, perhaps even the owners of the Roman state. But if that was ever true, those days were long past. Pompey had triumphed when not a senator and had once allowed the veterans of his Asian campaigns to take up positions in the senate to encourage it to vote the right way. Now his booty provided a dignified setting for its meetings. The senate had never regained its political prominence since the dictatorship of Sulla. Before that it had been locked in a struggle for sovereignty in the state with the Roman people, senatorial magistrates and decrees ranged against popular tribunes and the laws passed by their assemblies. Sulla had tried – not entirely unselfishly – to decide the matter in the senate's favour permanently. The laws he passed – the same laws his sometime lieutenants Pompey and Crassus abolished within a decade of his resignation of the dictatorship in 80 BC – had limited the power of the tribunes, traditional champions of the people, imposed minimum ages for high office, given senators the right to be tried by their peers instead of their social inferiors. But the means he had used to achieve this victory made it irrelevant. Sulla was the first general to persuade his troops to march on Rome. (He has the dubious distinction of being the only general to have flooded both the Roman forum and its Athenian equivalent, the agora, with blood.) The link Sulla fashioned between general and army, and the precedent established in bringing the army into the civil struggles in Rome, robbed senate and popular assemblies of any role other than to attempt to placate, flatter and control the generals.

These last decades of the Roman republic, when 'normal service' was so often and so bloodily interrupted, are those we see most clearly. The main reason is that we observe them through the eyes of Cicero, whose brilliant speeches – in political trials, to his fellow senators, even to the Roman citizen body – became instant classics of style and remained the basis of education in the west until the Renaissance and beyond. As well as the speeches we have a mass of his correspondence, including letters to Caesar, Brutus and all the great protagonists of his day as well as to intimate friends. From these, for example, we hear an eye-witness account of the spectacular vulgarity of the opening ceremonies for Pompey's theatre, a performance of a Greek tragedy with 600 mules among the extras, a battle of elephants ... Finally there is his scholarly writing on rhetoric and philosophy, especially ethics and particularly exercised by the political cataclysms of his day. What he has to say on tyrannicide will provide us with precious clues in the next chapter for how Caesar's murderers steeled themselves for their crime. And Cicero, the new man in the Roman senate, facing Caesar with his ancestors stretching back to Trojan Aeneas and his divine mother Venus, was forever the conservative defender of the senate's ancient (and perhaps imagined) prerogatives. His main political strategy was to unite the city (or the better portion of it) and to divide the generals: this radical innovation, in a city that had become great as a result of the competition for glory conducted by its warrior chiefs, was one born of desperation.

Mostly Cicero's 'consensus of all good men' failed. Pompey and Crassus had pooled their interests once before, in 70 BC. When Pompey returned from the east in 62 there was an attempt to marginalise him. The response was a new alliance to which Pompey and Crassus added a new partner, Gaius Julius Caesar. Son of an ancient patrician family, a darling of the populace rather than the senate, he brought to the junta priestly authority, oratorical flair and demagogic street cred. Together they intimidated the senate into giving them the commands they wanted, land to Pompey's soldiers and effective control of the major offices of the republic. Even when they fell out, the senate was powerless to regain control of the armies. During this time the great theatre rose, letting the people of Rome know where real power lay. Elephants for the masses, Greek art for a cultured elite, statuary that celebrated Roman conquest, cultural, political and military.

The magnificent theatre was completed in September or October 55 BC. That year the two chief magistracies of the state, the consulships, were held by Pompey and Crassus. Caesar was mid-way through the conquest of Gaul. His command there had been renewed for another five years by the senate, although the key moment had been a renewal of the pact between the three men in April the previous year, heading off an attempt by Cicero to break the alliance. The summer before Pompey's inaugural games Caesar had crossed the Channel to take Roman troops to Britain (or Across the Ocean) for the first time. Crassus was on the point of leaving Rome for a great campaign against the Parthian empire. The future seemed secure for the Big Three, and Rome's conquest of the world, powered by their rivalry, was proceeding faster than ever. Yet in just over a decade all were dead. Crassus had been slaughtered in battle on Rome's eastern frontier when his invasion of the Parthian empire ended in calamity. Pompey had been murdered by the Egyptian court in an effort to curry favour with Caesar, who had defeated him at Pharsalus, the conclusion of their brief civil war in 49–48 BC. And on 15 March 44 BC, Julius Caesar, the last of the three to survive, bled to death in the senate house of the great theatre at the feet of the statue of Pompey.

The biographer Suetonius tells the story:

As he took his seat, the conspirators gathered about him as if to pay their respects. At once Tillius Cimber, who had assumed the lead, came nearer as though to ask something; and when Caesar with a gesture put him off to another time, Cimber caught his toga by both shoulders; then as Caesar cried, 'Why, this is violence!' one of the Cascas stabbed him from one side just below the throat. Caesar caught Casca's arm and ran it through with his writing stylus, but as he tried to leap to his feet, he was stopped by another wound. When he saw that he was beset on every side by drawn daggers, he

5. *The Palazzo Spada Pompey, once believed to have been the very statue at the foot of which Caesar was murdered, this was used as a splendid prop when Voltaire's* La Mort de César *was performed in Rome.*

muffled his head in his robe, and at the same time drew down its lap to his feet with his left hand, in order to fall more decently, with the lower part of his body also covered. As he lay like this he was stabbed with twenty-three wounds, uttering not a word, but merely a groan at the first stroke, although some have written that when Marcus Brutus rushed at him, he said in Greek, 'You too, my child?'

What exactly happened there, in Pompey's senate house on the morning of the Ides of March 44 BC?

The main lines of the story are not at issue. Every ancient account describes how Caesar entered and took his seat. At the time of his death Caesar was not only Dictator, but now Dictator for Life, a title he had taken just a month before, and he was also one of the two consuls. The other was Mark Antony. Plutarch, who wrote a biography of Caesar almost a century and a half later, tells us that Antony was engaged in conversation outside the senate house by a conspirator. The meeting had not started. It was beginning a little late, perhaps around eleven in the morning, as Caesar had been delayed while performing sacrifice. Appian records that Brutus and Cassius had been there long before Caesar, doing business as praetors – the second most senior magistracy after the consuls – and exchanging words with other senators. Roman politics was all about networking: quiet words of support, favours asked and granted, snippets of information, gossip and rumour were the common currency. Friendships were maintained and reputations built by this hum of *sotto voce* transactions. More than once, Appian tells us, the nervous conspirators heard or misheard allusions to the plot as they waited.

When Caesar arrived, those already seated had risen to greet him. Romans rose to greet a superior, and were sensitive to breaches of etiquette. Caesar had given some offence only a few weeks before by failing to rise to greet the senate. When Brutus had unexpectedly taken Pompey's side in the civil war he had fought against Caesar, Pompey had risen to greet him 'as if he were his superior'. Now, four years later, Rome rose for Caesar.

Senators were obviously milling about. Now, before the meeting proper began, individuals would try to get in a word, pass a pleasantry, do a little quick business. Just like a large committee today before it is called to order. How many were present when the first blow was struck? The number of senators had swollen during the civil wars from around 300 before Sulla's dictatorship to 900 in 45 BC. Many had been appointed senators by Caesar. But not all were in Rome at the time of Caesar's death, not all senators attended every meeting (despite the rules), and presumably not all those due to attend on the Ides of March had yet entered the senate house. But there were certainly hundreds in the chamber already. Caesar himself was at the centre of a throng, surrounded by those he considered his allies: men like Brutus and Cassius, who as the urban and peregrine praetors respectively were the most senior magistrates in the city present after the two consuls, and Casca who was a tribune of the people and who struck the first blow. And as always Caesar was surrounded by a crowd of petitioners. Several accounts say Caesar received so many written petitions that he passed them to a slave to be considered later. Hundreds of anecdotes from the Roman empire describe the mass of letters showered upon emperors, magistrates and governors, asking for personal exemptions, for help in legal cases, for grants of office, money or support. Anecdotes about Caesar describe him signing letters over dinner and at the games. Since making himself master of Rome all depended on Caesar's will: future magistracies had been allocated years in advance. Great new building projects had been initiated. Caesar's good will might bring contracts. And then there were the pleas for political rehabilitation. Brutus was not the only great Roman to have fought on Pompey's losing side. Caesar's clemency was famous (and famously offensive since it was a virtue appropriate to a king). But Caesar's forgiveness was individualised, not general, and it had to be sought as a favour. There were so many reasons to crowd the dictator.

And suddenly a scuffle broke out. Most of those in the room must have been ignoring the familiar huddle around the seated Dictator. But in a moment the huddle turned into a scrum. There were screams – Caesar's voice called out at least once – then the cries of the conspirators, and brilliant white togas were splattered with scarlet blood. Twenty-three wounds, according to Suetonius. It had been agreed that every member of the party would stab Caesar at least once, according to Plutarch. In the confusion some conspirators stabbed each other. Only one wound was fatal, according to Antistius, whom Suetonius (who reports it) describes as a doctor. It must have been over in minutes, and no one ran to help Caesar.

Then panic. Brutus tried to make a speech, but most senators fled at once. No one knew who was in the conspiracy, nor who its targets were. Was a general bloodbath planned? How many of Caesar's supporters were also marked down for assassination? Caesar's two main deputies were Mark Antony and Marcus Lepidus. Lepidus was Master of Horse, the traditional second-in-command of a Dictator. Antony had held that position in 48 and 47. Now, with Caesar dead, he was the sole surviving consul. Both men fled to the houses of friends. Other senators scattered. Other accounts – those of Plutarch, Nicolaus and Dio – all relate how the panic spread through the city, shops and counters were abandoned, families bolted themselves up in their houses. The conspirators too abandoned the senate house. Suetonius claimed they had at first planned to drag Caesar's body and throw it into the Tiber (as if he were an executed criminal), but they changed their minds out of fear of Antony and Lepidus. How should they know the consul had fled for his life rather than summoned an avenging mob? Lepidus, in one account, had a legion of soldiers at his disposal on the Tiber island. The city was certainly full of veterans of Caesar's armies, men who had fought first Gauls and then fellow Romans under his command, some of them looking forward to new campaigns and the riches they would bring. But in the confusion, neither group could really have been deployed quickly. Quite possibly all sides were fleeing from each other within minutes of the murder. Incredibly, Caesar's body was apparently placed in his litter by three slaves and carried back to his home.

Meanwhile, a grisly procession found its way out of the senate house, across the Field of Mars and up on to the Capitol, the rocky hilltop overlooking the forum, the two summits of which were occupied by the temple of Jupiter and the Citadel surrounded by a host of lesser temples. The conspirators marched through the empty streets waving their bloodstained daggers with pride, calling out that liberty had been restored. A few sympathisers joined them en route. But if they had expected to be hailed by the masses as liberators, they were disappointed. At first things went well. A speech by Brutus on the Capitol was well received, and he and the others were (according to most accounts) escorted by a crowd of senators down the processional way into the forum to the rostrum, the platform used by speakers to address the crowd. A second speech by Brutus went well enough, but when one of the other conspirators, Cinna, started on the subject of Caesar the crowd turned ugly. Frightened at this development, the conspirators retreated back to the Capitol. Some of those who had joined them after the murder melted away. The spring afternoon grew colder. Night fell.

The details, of course, vary from one account to another. And we have many accounts. But the fullest narratives that survive today were written long after the Ides of March. Plutarch, a Greek philosopher writing in the late first and early second centuries AD, wrote moralizing biographies of Brutus and Antony, Caesar and Cicero, all of which touch on the conspiracy. Just a little later is Suetonius's *Life of the Deified Julius*, the first in a series of twelve Latin imperial biographies composed in the comfort of the court of Hadrian, where the author was a scholar and official. Two more Greek narratives are even later, that of the Alexandrian historian Appian, perhaps written under Hadrian's successor Antoninus Pius, whose long reign straddled the middle of the second century AD, and another by Cassius Dio, a senator serving under the Severan dynasty at the end of the century. Appian and Dio were already writing ancient history the way we do today, comparing the written accounts they found in great libraries, that is. But Dio writes as a senator looking back to the origins of the empire, while Appian, a man of lower rank, describes it near the end of his long account of the civil wars that brought about the fall of the Roman republic. A few others mention the murder only in passing: Velleius, whose main aim was to glorify the second emperor, Tiberius, is an example. Only Cicero is a contemporary witness and he offers no connected account of the events. Nicolaus of Damascus, a courtier of the first emperor Augustus, spoke to eye-witnesses. But only fragments of his account, and of that of his contemporary Livy, survive. And echoes of the event of the Ides of March rumbled through Roman literature from Sallust's account of the senator Catiline's abortive coup in 63 BC, in which a youthful Caesar had perhaps played a part, to Lucan's great epic poem on Caesar's civil war with Pompey, written at the court of Nero. Behind most of these accounts are others, now lost, themselves based on the confused rumours and interested oral versions of the various players in the drama. Almost no fact is certain, or undisputed.

How did Caesar react when attacked? Suetonius had read some accounts that said Caesar lay silent under the rain of blows and others that had him reproach Brutus with his last breath. Plutarch too had read several versions: some, he writes, say that Caesar fought back until he saw Brutus approach dagger drawn, and then gave up the fight. Dio too had read differing versions: those he described as most reliable claimed Caesar had said no word, but others claimed he greeted Brutus with 'You too, my son?' just as Suetonius said. Appian gives a blow-by-blow account of the fight in which Caesar defends himself fiercely until wounded by Brutus. He alone says that some senators and innocent bystanders were killed in the stampede to escape.

How many conspirators were there? Nicolaus says there were more than eighty, Suetonius says there were sixty, yet if Plutarch is right that each conspirator stabbed Caesar once, the total should be twenty-three. (Livy agrees there were twenty-three blows, but Nicolaus says there were thirty-five.) Appian lists just fifteen names. And who was the instigator of the plot? Plutarch and Appian have Cassius recruiting Brutus, but Dio portrays Brutus as the first conspirator.

Other differences are trivial. Was it Trebonius who engaged Antony in conversation outside the senate house, or Decimus Brutus Albinus? Appian and Dio say Trebonius, and Plutarch gives both names, one in his life of Brutus, the other in his life of Caesar. Appian alone has Tillius Cimber cry out, 'Why do you delay, my friends?' as he pulled Caesar's toga down to expose his neck. Which Brutus was it who persuaded Caesar to attend the senate meeting? Decimus Brutus as most accounts say, or Marcus Junius Brutus, the leader of the conspiracy as Nicolaus seems to think? The accounts that Plutarch and Appian give of the speeches made to the people by Cinna and Brutus from the rostrum differ in almost every detail.

Different accounts also have different emphases. Plutarch presents the conspirators' march up on to the Capitol, the old citadel that loomed over the Roman forum, as a triumphant declaration of their deeds, and their retreat there from the forum as the liberators seeking refuge from a mob. His Brutus is nearly always noble, even if Cassius is regarded as less honourable. Velleius Paterculus, on the other hand, like Dio, writes entirely from the side of Caesar and represents the assassination as a ghastly crime. He presents the conspirators as seizing the Capitol with the help of a band of gladiators belonging to Decimus Brutus. Plutarch notes the existence of the gladiators as one reason why Decimus Brutus was recruited to the conspiracy but gives them no role in his narrative. In Appian's account the gladiators had been armed to perform in Pompey's theatre and rushed into the senate house in the confusion, then escorted the conspirators on to the Capitol. Appian in general is much more sensitive to the masses of soldiery on the fringe of these events. As well as the troops commanded in the city by Lepidus, Caesar's Master of Horse, and the gladiators on the Capitol, there were the veterans of Caesar's legions prowling the city. Only a few days' march away was the army of Cisalpine Gaul, the great province in the Po Valley which had been Caesar's for eight years, now assigned to Decimus Brutus. Which way would they jump? Accounts of the immediate aftermath are especially jumbled, as troops moved about the city by dark and the leaders of the city visited each others' houses and sent messages as they tried to agree on how to break the deadlock. Some writers seem to think the senate met the next day, on 16 March, although it is pretty certain it was not until the 17th that Antony summoned a meeting in the temple of the goddess Tellus, in the district of Rome known as the Carinae.

None of these discrepancies are serious. It is easy enough for historians to reconcile minor differences, to suggest sources of confusion or even to rank historians in terms of their reliability so as to produce an homogenised and consistent account. Modern accounts sometimes claim to be superior precisely because they do combine details from many different sources, and correct the errors and misunderstandings in each. But this conventional tactic misses the point. Both Suetonius and Plutarch go out of their way to stress that they too had found contradictory accounts in *their* sources, most of which are now lost to us but some of which were written very close to the events themselves. What had really happened was shrouded in uncertainty from the start.

All the surviving narratives look back to a mass of accounts written very soon after the events. There survive a number of letters written by Cicero between Caesar's murder and his own, just eighteen months later, which give vivid flashes of the panic and uncertainty of the day. The speech Cicero made on 2 September offers an account of what went wrong after the success of the conspiracy, which he supported after the event, as well as an excuse for his own actions. Similarly interested texts written a little later deal with the part played by Caesar's heir, Marcus Octavius, who was adopted in Caesar's will as Gaius Julius Caesar Octavianus and became the Emperor Augustus after two more rounds of vicious civil war. But the first accounts of the assassination itself are now lost. Brutus's friend the Greek rhetorician Empylus wrote a *Brutus* which described the assassination. Brutus's stepson, Bibulus, wrote *Memoirs of Bibulus*: some at least of the vivid accounts of the bravery of Brutus's wife Porcia derive from this. Was Antistius' claim that only one wound had been fatal made in another pamphlet? Plutarch had read letters Brutus had written to Cicero after the murder and the memoirs or history of Publius Volumnius, who accompanied Brutus on the campaigns that led to his death after the battle of Philippi in 42 BC. Plutarch found accounts of the suicide of Brutus's wife in the work of the historian-philosopher Nicolaus of Damascus and in Valerius Maximus's account of *Memorable Deeds and Words*. The latter was himself a compiler, dependent on other sources: did this story come from a letter of Cicero? Or from Livy's history (lost for these years)? But then everyone was writing about Caesar and Brutus.

Behind the mass of diverging accounts of Caesar's death must lie even more verbal accounts. Hundreds were present at the murder. Yet few were paying attention to the action, which was over in a minute. Almost no one, not even the perpetrators, can have got a clear view. Shouts and cries would have drowned out the actual words spoken. Panic, flight, shame and for some a desire to share in the glory must have distorted the first accounts given, to relatives, friends, senators outside the building. After the first terror, there must have been an intense hunger for news. Cicero at once dashed off a short note to one conspirator, Lucius Minucius Basilus, which ran as follows.

> Congratulations! I rejoice. I adore you and have your interests at heart. I hope for your love in return and want to know what you are doing and what is being done.

The news spread further and further afield. Nicolaus has a vivid account of how word of Caesar's death was sent to Octavius by his mother Atia through a letter carried by a trusted ex-slave. Octavius was studying in the Greek city of Apollonia, on the other side of the Adriatic. The conspiracy was large, Octavius was told, and all Caesar's relatives were in danger. Almost at once rumours spread through the city. Octavius debated his best course with his friends and with prominent locals. Should he try to get the local legions of Macedonia to march on Rome to avenge his great-uncle? He decided instead to set off for Rome without troops. Crossing the Adriatic, he arrived in the remote Italian town of Lupiae, where news of Caesar's murder was not yet common knowledge. But some of those there had been in Rome, and could tell him that Caesar's will had been read out, that Octavius was his heir and that Brutus and Cassius were in possession of the Capitol and promising the slaves freedom if they joined them. More rumours were followed by more letters from Atia. Caesar's veterans had flooded the city. The conspirators had been granted safe passage out of Rome down the coast to the city of Antium. Their houses in Rome were under siege. The populace had turned against them. As Octavius approached Rome cautiously, from Lupiae to Brindisi, then overland along the Appian Way, more friends and information arrived. Nicolaus's account presumably contains some genuine reminiscences and some spin. But the story of news and rumours spreading together, the jumbled chronology of events, the uncertainty over the balance of power and level of threat, are completely plausible.

As always happens, chaotic events set loose a chaotic tangle of stories, the remains of which present themselves to us as a contradictory and confused mass of written evidence. Different versions spread out from the events themselves like the blood from Caesar's twenty-three puncture wounds. No definitive version of events could ever be established. Only as the new order of things settled in did it become possible to fix a pattern around events, and more than one pattern was available. The first choice was whether to write the story as a tyrannicide carried out reluctantly for noble ends, nothing less than the restoration of liberty. Another was to portray it as a vicious crime perpetrated for their own ends by those who pretended to be Caesar's friends and owed their lives and positions to him. That debate had begun before Caesar's corpse was cold.

⚏

At dawn on 17 March, not two full days after Caesar's death, the senate was convened in the temple of Tellus. Why there? Because the senate house attached to Pompey's theatre was obviously inappropriate and because the main senate house was in the forum, just below the Capitol and next to the stations taken up by Lepidus's troops. The temple of Tellus was more than 200 years old but had been rebuilt just a decade ago, around the same time as Pompey's theatre, so was probably fairly capacious. It was also very close to Antony's house – formerly Pompey's house as it happened – and it was Antony, as consul, who convened the meeting, along with Dolabella, the man whom Caesar had already designated to replace him once he left Rome on the planned campaign against the Parthian empire. The constitutionality of Dolabella's succession was dubious, and the senate might equally have been convened by Lepidus as Master of Horse or even Brutus as the senior praetor, but in the circumstances these were the least of the senate's worries. The meeting had, naturally, been preceded by intense diplomacy, and there was a script. Cicero made a speech. All accounts (his own included) agree that he recommended that the Romans follow the precedent set by the Athenians in 403 BC. After the defeat of Athens at the end of the Peloponnesian War, an oligarchic faction had been installed by the Spartan victors. It was soon overthrown, by a mixture of democratic protest and exiles returning with foreign support, but the Athenians resolved to grant the oligarchs an amnesty rather than plunge the state into more civil discord. Cicero proposed the same, that civil strife be forgotten. Antony supported the proposal. So did Munatius Plancus, another prominent Caesarian lieutenant who had been praetor the previous year. Caesar's acts were not to be repealed, but the conspirators were to face no punishment, indeed their actions were to be the object of a formal vote of thanks. The motion was passed.

More diplomacy followed through the day of 17 March. Antony and Lepidus sent their children to the Capitol as hostages, the conspirators eventually descended and there were meetings in Antony's house. Brutus dined that night with Lepidus, and Cassius with Antony. The senate met again the next day to ratify the concordat. Antony was praised. Brutus, Cassius and the other senators were praised. The office of dictator which Caesar had held was abolished for ever. The senate then allotted provinces to the main conspirators for the following year, 43. Roman provinces were governed by retiring magistrates. Traditionally the senate allocated them on the basis of the current needs of the empire, but that allocation had often been fiercely contentious in the recent past, and it was a pragmatic move to guarantee those conspirators concerned that revenge would not be taken on them by the senate when the allocation was made. Finally it was agreed that Caesar should receive a public funeral in the forum, the traditional honour given to the greatest Roman nobles.

⌛

Conspiracy, the murder of the chief magistrate, panic and flight, battle lines drawn between forum and Capitol, and it ends like this? With reconciliation, dinner parties and praises all round? That the leaders of Rome could even imagine letting bygones be bygones seems incredible to us. Of course it failed. Ahead lay the flight of the conspirators, the massing of armies on either side, the murder of Cicero by the soldiers of Antony and Octavian, the vengeance they took for Caesar from Brutus and Cassius on the battlefield of Philippi in northern Greece, the suicides of the two main conspirators, and then a new uneasy compact between the victors, followed by cold war and proxy wars fought by their friends, leading on to the eventual defeat of Antony at Actium in 31 BC and a sole rule by Octavian, becoming Augustus, that was far more monarchical and absolute than anything Caesar had ever attempted to impose. The human cost of that thirteen-year detour from one monarchy to another was staggering: aristocrats were hunted down and slaughtered, Roman soldiers clashed with Roman soldiers in bloody battles, allies were drawn in on both sides, provincial cities and neighbouring kingdoms were casually despoiled and destroyed. But all that is for later. For the moment the question is this. How could the Roman aristocracy – the senate really – move so swiftly from business as normal to political murder, and back to even a show of normality?

Understanding the place of violence in Roman politics requires a massive imaginative effort on our part. We are used, after all, to two kinds of political system. Liberal democracies across the modern world have many variations, but they share enough of a political culture that we can recognise in each the interplay of party politics and personalities, the tension between government and parliament, the use of speeches and the power of silent influence, and so on. Leaders rise and fall in relation to their ability to dominate their own party and to enable their party to dominate the government. Reputations can be damaged in ways that lead to rapid falls from grace. Political invective and the manipulation of scandals are powerful weapons. But actual violence is very rare. So much for the civilised worlds we inhabit. Then there are the other political systems, those characterised by the periodic entry of the military into politics, by the prohibition of alternative political parties, interference in elections, and by censorship, house arrest, imprisonment, torture and the murder of opposition politicians or critics of the government. The idea that any of these conditions might be normal or permanent, let alone that violence might be used to create order, is horrifying to us.

Yet the Roman republic seems to straddle these two worlds. Governed by rules and conventions that, if not precisely the same as ours, at least allow us to speak of constitutionality, it was also given to paroxysms of violence. Even more bizarre, the political classes were willing to do the dirty work themselves. Take the method of assassination. Modern assassins typically come from outside the political classes, even in states prone to chronic violence. Secret policemen, the military, veterans, criminal elements or even foreign mercenaries are employed to do the dirty work. Yet Brutus and Cassius did not make use of their slaves, of which they owned many, nor soldiers, many of whom had served with them under Pompey's command in the recent war against Caesar. Instead they carried out the murder themselves. Nor was this unprecedented. Tiberius Gracchus, a tribune of the plebs who in 133 BC had challenged what the senate considered its prerogatives, had been murdered by a mob of senators, some of them his close relations. Between then and Caesar's death there had been several similar killings.

Sulla's march on Rome in 88 BC had brought the army into politics. It lurked as an ugly shadow around even those conspiracies that were stifled at birth. Sulla also invented the practice of proscribing a list of his enemies, all prominent Romans: the proscribed could be killed with impunity and their property was forfeit to the state, which auctioned it off to other members of the aristocracy. And in 63 BC Cicero, as consul, executed without trial a group of nobles implicated in a botched coup attempt, an attempt that he alleged was to begin with the murder of the consuls. Yet in between these violent episodes the assemblies met as normal, elected magistrates and priests, voted on war and peace and other legislation, and the senate was regularly convened to discuss foreign and domestic matters, to issue edicts, to allocate provincial commands and decide on religious matters. Collected together in one temple or another, dressed in their formal togas, senators gave their views in strict precedence and debated with colleagues who, in other circumstances, they might have tried to kill with their own hands.

Even some ancient commentators seem to have found the interpenetration of violence and aristocratic concern with constitutional niceties bizarre. Think of the dinners that bracket Caesar's death. The night of 13 March he dined with Lepidus, his deputy as dictator. Among the other guests was Decimus Brutus, who the next morning would play a key role in encouraging Caesar to ignore bad omens and attend the planned senate meeting. Again on the night of the 17th Cassius was Antony's guest. After the meal, says Dio, Antony asked him if he had a concealed dagger about him there and then, and Cassius responded, 'Indeed I have, if you get any idea of making yourself tyrant.'

The calm with which the state was – albeit briefly – put back together after the murder of Caesar can be explained in various ways.

One tactic, already tried by some ancient writers, is to attribute the compromise to the power of vested interests. So Antony's decision to treat with the conspirators might be explained by his fear that Lepidus, who already had troops in the city, might exploit the situation to make himself dictator.

Peace would prevent him resorting to violence, and would compel the senate to throw their weight behind Antony as the surviving consul in the name of constitutionality. Cicero's interest was always in consensus, where he could lead. The conspirators had decide not to recruit him, which allowed him to play the role of broker. One account had Antony persuade the senate not to annul Caesar's acts on the grounds that many of them had been allocated praetorships, consulships and provinces in advance by the dictator. If Caesar's acts were annulled they would have to compete again, at great expense and with no guarantee of success. As for Brutus and Cassius, it really does seem that they had no programme beyond tyrannicide, and they too hoped for provinces. Lepidus would not be tyrant, but inherited the senior priesthood vacated by Caesar's death, and he too had a province to go on to.

The Roman republican political system was characterised by an extreme distribution of prestige and rotation of power among the elite. By 43 BC there were two consulships, sixteen praetorships and a host of minor magistracies of which the aedileships and the quaestorships were most important, and often early stages in a career. Each magistracy was held for just one year and repeating a magistracy was rare. Magistracies were always organised in colleges, and one magistrate could often cancel out the action of his colleague. Only in exceptional circumstances was a sole magistrate elected – either an interrex (an official appointed to organise elections if both consuls were dead), or a dictator to lead the state in time of military emergency. Used repeatedly in the darkest days of the war against Hannibal, when Romans contemplated utter defeat, it was this latter position that first Sulla and then Caesar used to cloak their domination of the state with constitutional language. Pompey had briefly served as sole consul for similar reasons. The tribunes of the people were not strictly magistrates but like them were elected: they could veto legislation and intercede for any citizen before a magistrate as well as convening popular assemblies.

Roman constitutional myth held that these elaborate checks and balances were devised as a protection against tyranny of the kind exercised by the last king of Rome. Rome had, it was believed, been ruled at first by a series of kings. Some were revered as founding fathers, but the last kings had behaved like tyrants and it was their expulsion (by the first Brutus) that was remembered as the origins of the republic, with its senate, assemblies, consuls, praetors and all the rest. Roman historians knew matters were more complicated and less certain, and many scholars today have even greater doubts about the historicity of the accounts of regal Rome penned in Cicero's day. But the myth of a republic founded on the expulsion of the kings was as powerful in Caesar's lifetime as the myth of the Pilgrim Fathers or Magna Carta remains today. By the last century BC, some Romans regarded constitutional conventions and laws as guarantees against a new kind of tyranny, an assurance that the aristocracy and the rich would respect the rights and persons of the commons. In practice these rules worked to keep the political class broad, to ensure a high level of political participation among the Roman aristocracy and to strengthen the position of the senate. Holding any magistracy gave life membership of the senate, subject only to remaining wealthy and of relatively good character, a test applied by a pair of magistrates named censors elected every five years. The result was that a Roman aristocrat might be a senator for thirty years or more, but serve as a magistrate for probably no more than three or four of them, and perhaps only once, since not everyone made it to the consulship. Typically the posts were held in a set sequence – one which Sulla had tried but failed to prescribe entirely. So Caesar himself, born in 100 BC, was quaestor in 68 BC, aedile five years later, praetor in 62 BC and consul (at the age of forty-one) in 59 BC. During a year of office the magistrates were prominent in the public eye as well as busy in the senate. They performed sacrifices, addressed the people at assemblies and some of them gave spectacular games. Caesar's own games had been held on an unprecedented scale.

Another way to stay in the public eye was to be elected to a priesthood, of which there were dozens. Priests too were organised in colleges, they were generally senators and they usually served for life. Caesar was elected Flamen Dialis, the priest of Jupiter, in 84 when he was just sixteen years old. Unusually he did not hold the position for life, but was elected a member of the college of pontiffs in 73 and then chief pontiff (the position Lepidus was to inherit from him) in 63. These honours and titles mattered enormously in Roman society, where public ceremonial, formal precedence and subtle gradations of rank were valued highly as marks of one's worth, for which the Latin term was *dignitas*. When explaining why he had crossed the Rubicon in 49 and marched against Pompey rather than dismissing his troops as the senate had ordered, one of Caesar's explanations was that he owed it to his *dignitas*. The idea that protecting one's public valuation was an adequate excuse for starting a civil war is another reminder of the gulf between Roman values and our own. Consider too the prominence given in the concordat to maintaining the face of all parties. Antony had to have his vote of thanks and so did the conspirators, however inconsistent it might seem. Even murdered Caesar had to have his public funeral to avoid disturbing the delicate economy of prestige.

There were tangible benefits to office too. Magistrates, especially the praetors and consuls, had from the beginning combined in their persons civil and military authority. Once upon a time the two consuls might in their year of office open the new year, preside over the senate, convene assemblies, organise the elections and also raise a citizen levy, lead the army and return home to celebrate their victories before laying down their office. The management of the empire had grown out of this system. As Rome acquired overseas territories it assigned their government first to magistrates and then to the previous year's office holders (termed promagistrates). Holding a senior magistracy by the first century BC was as important for the province that would follow as for the power and prestige it conveyed in itself.

If we look at the principal actors in the drama of 17 March 44 BC we can see a map of the Roman empire in their actual and promised provinces. Lepidus had been promised the province of nearer Spain. Decimus Brutus already had the governorship of rich Cisalpina. Munatius Plancus, who joined the advocates of reconciliation, was scheduled to take over the vast province of non-Mediterranean Gaul that Caesar had conquered in the fifties. Under the terms of the next day's settlement Brutus was assigned Crete and Cassius the rich province of Africa, Trebonius Asia and Tillius Cimber Bithynia. The very fact that the conspiracy had originated among and divided the highest magistrates of the state meant that conspirators and their opponents alike had interests in the status quo. The experience of central and eastern Europe following the collapse of the Soviet bloc provides plenty of close parallels. Bizarre as it seems, immediate reconciliation suited the interests of most of the major players.

But interest-based analysis tells only part of the story. It is still worth asking how members of the senate could bring themselves to behave as if the assassination had not taken place. What pre-political urges and less rational forces were at work?

One obvious factor was fear, in particular fear that the conflict would escalate. Catiline's plot, the suppression of which in 63 was the high point of Cicero's consulship (and in his own eyes of his career), provides an instructive analogy. Rumours of a coup had been circulating for years, including rumours of an aborted attempt the previous year. Modern and ancient interpretations have been heavily influenced by Cicero's own version(s) of events, which sought first to demonise and exaggerate the threat, then to sing his own praises and sometimes to justify the summary executions which later returned to haunt him and even drove him briefly into exile. How many were involved, what their objects were and how far they would have gone is now obscure. But Cicero was able to carry the senate with him, Catiline did flee the city and this was followed by an armed insurrection in Etruria, so the threat was certainly real. What neither Cicero nor his main chronicler Sallust make clear, however, is that one reason Cicero was allowed to act as he did by the senate was that the events took place while Pompey was in command of a vast Roman army in the eastern Mediterranean. Most senators over forty – all the ex-consuls for example – would remember a disturbing parallel from just eighteen years before. Then it had been Sulla leading the Roman forces against Mithridates, also in Asia, when news had reached him that the measures he had set in place after capturing Rome had been reversed and that his enemies now controlled the city. Sulla wound up the war rapidly – too rapidly perhaps – and his return was terrible. Whatever the senate in 63 thought of Catiline, they were prepared to go to great lengths to avoid Pompey imitating his master. Twenty years on again, in March 44, many senators would have been acutely conscious of the dangers of escalation. With almost all the protagonists going to armed provinces in the next few months, the risk of another bloodbath perhaps made reconciliation the lesser evil.

To fear add affection, jealousy, family solidarity and old rivalries. There are politicians today, especially in smaller countries or regional politics, who have known one another since childhood or early adulthood, who are connected by long-standing friendships or business connections or in a few cases by family ties and marriage. But in most cases their relationships with each other are formed primarily through common participation in political life. The Roman republic was quite different. It is not just that there were no professional political classes, although that was true, as in all ancient states. But Roman senators were drawn overwhelmingly from a narrow world of families densely connected with each other through marriage, patronage, education and even just physical propinquity. That political world seems terribly claustrophobic to us. Brutus was married to the daughter of the Cato who had ended his career as a Pompeian general. She was also his cousin, and the widow of the man who had been Caesar's colleague as consul in 59 BC. Brutus's mother (Cato's sister) had been Caesar's mistress. Brutus and Lepidus were brothers-in-law. Caesar himself was related through his aunt to Marius, Sulla's great enemy, and his daughter married Pompey during the fifties. After her death Pompey married the daughter of Metellus Scipio, a man whose name itself bears the trace of a dynastic connection between two powerful families. Although young, she was already the widow of Caesar's former ally Crassus. It would be easy to multiply examples. Notoriously these connections cut across political groupings. When Tiberius Gracchus was killed by a mob of senators, both his followers and those attacking him included close relatives.

Not all families belonged to this exclusive club. Civil wars and their aftermath had done terrible damage to some old families by the time of the dictatorship of Caesar. More importantly, the massive expansion of the senate under Caesar had brought in rich members of communities up and down Italy, some of them the children of Italians who had fought against Roman armies to win enfranchisement just a generation before. These new arrivals had no senatorial ancestors, typically they collected fewer magistracies and priesthoods, and many would fail to establish their own descendants in the senate. Cicero's success had been truly unusual, a mark of his exceptional talent. These families are not prominent in the dramas of 44 BC. Virtually all the main players belonged to that inner circle where social credentials, breeding, culture and political office were assumed to be concentrated. Members of these families helped each other out almost by instinct. Patronage of this sort extended bonds of obligation and alliance out beyond the family to friends and the children of friends. Caesar, while commanding in Gaul, gave positions on his staff to younger relatives of both Crassus and Cicero. Candidates for office might depend on a senior figure offering his support in the elections. Cicero supplied testimonials for his friends. Perhaps in earlier times a loose reciprocity between families had ensured that these favours were returned, if only in the next generation. But from the fifties BC more and more magistracies and commands were effectively in the gift of Pompey, Crassus and Caesar, and finally of Caesar alone. Hence the deluge of petitions. Acts of patronage enhanced the *dignitas* of the giver and, like acts of clemency, put the recipient under an obligation. But the obligations Caesar created could never adequately be repaid.

Other connections formed within this inner group. The importance of age in structuring a Roman career meant that adolescents of the right families might well find themselves being educated together and then passing together through the same rites of passage, the taking of the toga of manhood, military service, competition for the minor offices, then for higher magistracies and so on. And the real elite shared a common culture. Caesar with his last breath and Casca striking the first blow are both said to have called out in Greek. Cicero appealed to Athenian precedent when advocating an amnesty for the conspirators and general reconciliation. The Greek masterpieces in Pompey's theatre were echoed by Cicero's own more modest collection in his rural retreat at Tusculum, where he spent much of Caesar's dictatorship composing philosophical works based on Greek texts. His letters to Brutus, Caesar, Plancus and above all his friend Atticus are peppered with Greek quotations and Greek words. This fascination for a particular kind of Greek culture was part of the common cultural currency of the innermost elite.

Finally, propinquity. The Romans were a people who inhabited a single state and one great city within it. Romans often referred to Rome simply as the City, and Livy wrote his great history with the title *From the Foundation of the City*. Romans all belonged to a single state. (Greeks by contrast were divided among many autonomous cities, and each one typically sheltered some of its neighbours' exiled leaders, waiting for a change in the political wind that would allow them to return.) For Romans, however, exile was a terrible punishment. Occasionally an aristocrat might withdraw to a colony, as one Scipio did to Liternum in the Bay of Naples when the state would not recognise, as he saw it, his claims to be treated differently in respect of his military achievements. Those were the days! Cicero and Sallust both looked back nostalgically to the Rome of the Scipios, in which great generals served the state rather than destroyed it. One of Cicero's opponents, Verres, lived out his life in comfortable exile in the Greek city of Marseilles, but he was effectively removed from the board of Roman politics as a result. Rome was, for most aristocrats, the only show in town. Indeed the most ancient families lived virtually on top of each other. The house of a Roman aristocrat was a powerful symbol of his status and often of his ancestry. Cult was paid in the entrance hall to the Lares and Penates of the family, busts of ancestors were stored and sometimes displayed, a few had painted family trees on the walls or inscriptions advertising the achievements of the clan. Ceremonies and even family courts were convened before these symbols of past greatness. One account of the Ides of March has the conspirators meet at Cassius's house to celebrate his son taking on the toga of manhood, before walking down to the senate house together. The world inhabited by the rulers of the Mediterranean was physically tiny, however broad their cultural horizons. Some houses were ancestral mansions, some acquired from great predecessors, many had been elaborately rebuilt in the preceding century thanks to the spoils of empire, many bore trophies or insignia testifying to their occupants' great deeds. The night before Caesar's death his wife Calpurnia was said to have dreamt that a great architectural ornament bestowed on Caesar's house by the senate had collapsed. Although the population of the city in 44 BC was between half a million and a million souls, the greatest families all lived in the very centre. Recent excavations have uncovered great archaic mansions on the forum side of the Palatine. Cicero lived on the Palatine, Antony on the Carinae, others elsewhere on the lower slopes of the hills of Rome. When the senators fled the theatre of Pompey to their homes it was an obvious move, since most of their houses were less than half a mile away.

One reason the Roman elite did recover – repeatedly – from the acts of violence and betrayal their members inflicted on each other during the late republic was that this was the only world they had. The intensely urban nature of their society meant they could not retire to their rural seats like medieval barons. The fact that there was only one Roman city meant they would not go so gently into exile as others. But theirs was no culture of forgiveness. Sulla boasted that no one had done as much as he had to help his friends or harm his enemies. A great temple to Avenging Mars was vowed by Octavian and Mark Antony if the god helped them track down and punish the conspirators: he did, and the temple eventually constructed became the centrepiece of the Forum of Augustus, that monumental complex that was in some ways the first emperor's answer to the theatre of Pompey, but one where the statues were of great Romans not of Greek myths, and that advertised Augustus's role as the new monarch of Rome, the descendant of three gods, Venus, Mars and the Deified Julius Caesar himself.

But for most republican aristocrats who survived civil war, riots and proscription, revenge had to wait, and civilised customs had in the meantime to be observed. The price of remaining in the game until an opportunity for revenge presented itself was to go to the senate house as normal, to walk calmly through the forum, to attend sacrifices and banquets and meetings of priestly colleges, all in the company of your once and future mortal enemies. Amazingly, most of the Roman elite in the days after Caesar's death were prepared to pay this price. The people, and Caesar's former soldiers, however, were not.

⧗

Maybe if it had been left to the Roman aristocracy they could have weathered the storm. But it was not. As the conspirators had discovered within hours of killing Caesar, the Roman populace was not prepared to hail them as liberators. No surprise, perhaps, since the freedom for which Brutus and Cassius had fought was the freedom of the senate. The population of Rome had suffered no real restrictions under the dictatorship except the loss of the liberty to elect magistrates.

A temporary loss of political freedom maybe mattered less to the Roman people since Caesar's first power base had been the so-called popular party. During the seventy years that separated the murder of the popular tribune Tiberius Gracchus from the summary execution without trial of Catiline's alleged confederates by Cicero, a set of slogans and policies had developed which stressed the sovereignty of the Roman people over the rights that nobility and senate claimed were theirs by ancestry. Successive politicians, all senators and often from the oldest nobility, as both Gracchus and Caesar were, used the assemblies and the tribunate to circumvent and control senate and magistrates. We know that the label *popularis* (popular) was attached to those who espoused these views and used these tactics, because Cicero once attempted to steal their clothes by claiming (to a popular assembly of course) to be a true *popularis*, on the grounds that his policies were those that really served the interests of the people best. Later Greek writers found no difficulty in treating the Roman republic as divided into two parties, but although individual *populares* were often connected by kinship, and most proposed similar policies about land reform, colonisation or electoral reform, in practice they were a disparate group. Being a *popularis* was more of a strategy, a choice of rhetorical weaponry, a decision to align oneself with one group of friends and relatives rather than another. Caesar made this choice early in his career, partly because his connections made him well placed to do so, partly perhaps because Sulla's enmity made the opposite course more difficult to follow.

The weight of this tangled history weighed heavily on all parties to the Ides of March and their aftermath. Caesar's first wife was the daughter of Cinna, the consul who had seized Rome during Sulla's absence in the east. Caesar's aunt had married Sulla's enemy Marius, the popular hero who had been first promoted and then shunned by his noble backers and had ended his career allied to the successors of the murdered Gracchi brothers. Caesar had been made priest of Jupiter by Marius and Cinna: he had had to flee Sulla as a result. As he campaigned for magistracies and priesthoods through the seventies and sixties, in an age when all major players were distancing themselves from the former dictator, he made the most of these credentials. But it could be dangerous. Some thought him implicated in Catiline's *popularis* plot in 63. And to court the people he would need more than his brilliant oratory. Caesar spent extravagantly on games and public shows whenever possible. As aedile in 65 BC, two years before standing for election as chief priest, he gave spectacular games and put on 320 pairs of gladiators, supposedly as funeral games for his father who had died twenty years before. The scale was unprecedented and the cost extravagant: Caesar was said to have quipped, as he went out for the pontifical elections, that if he were not successful he would have to go into exile to escape his creditors. His opponents were worried at the popularity he was winning. There was even an attempt to ban from elections those who had given shows in the preceding two years.

Caesar was absent from Rome for most of the fifties, conquering Gaul and invading Britain and Germany, but he sent frequent dispatches back in which – to judge from the published war *Commentaries* – the deeds of ordinary Roman soldiers were advertised more prominently than those of their aristocratic leaders. Those citizens who served in his Gallic Wars were richly rewarded. Caesar too was enriched, paid off his debts and began to spend politically. The year after the dedication of Pompey's theatre, Caesar began planning a rival piazza complex just next door on the Field of Mars. The Saepta Julia was to be another great porticoed monument of marble, again decorated with statue groups. At 310 by 130 metres in dimension, it was minutely larger than Pompey's complex. Significantly, given Caesar's popular credentials, it was also designed as a venue for the assemblies to vote.

At the same time work began on a great basilica, a covered hall along the southern side of the forum. The people were not the only group to enjoy games and appreciate the monumentalisation of the city, but Caesar worked hard to give his projects a popular twist that those of other aristocrats, Pompey in particular, lacked.

As dictator, Caesar continued to provide entertainments and to build. Four days in late July were earmarked for games in honour of the victory over Pompey at Pharsalus (although they were tactfully dedicated to his ancestor Venus). Later, in 46, there were triumphs over Egypt, Pontus and Africa, with more spectacular games to accompany them. Suetonius writes:

> After the triumphs, he distributed rewards to his soldiers, and treated the people with feasting and shows. He entertained the entire people together at one feast, where twenty-two thousand dining couches were laid out; and he made a display of gladiators, and of battles by sea, in honour, as he said, of his daughter Julia, though she had been long since dead.

Meanwhile a new senate house was to be built, a new forum with a temple of Venus at its centre and much more. Most spectacular was Caesar's building in the Circus Maximus, the great chariot-racing track in the long valley between the Palatine hill and the Aventine. Its capacity was expanded to accommodate 150, 000 spectators, they were given stone seating where before they had sat on temporary stands or on the grass, and a great moat was added separating the audience from the track so that wild animal hunts could be safely organised inside it. In a Rome that did not yet have a Colosseum or any other amphitheatre, the Circus was *the* monument to games, festivals and their most extravagant funder. Great harbour works were planned at the port of Rome. Most of Caesar's building projects were unfinished at the time of his murder, but his would-be successors took care to complete them.

Caesar was no mere demagogue. During his brief dictatorship he made real attempts to deal with some of Rome's long-standing problems. Supplying the city with enough food, and avoiding the riots caused by fluctuations in the price of grain, had been an issue since the middle of the second century. Caesar set about designing a system that went beyond gratifying his supporters, including subsidies, infrastructure investment and a new system of managing it. The city itself was bursting at the seams as migrants had flowed into the capital. To reduce the population pressure, and to provide for the veterans of foreign and civil wars, he initiated a great campaign of colonisation around the Mediterranean. The land, the grain supply, colonisation – all these were old *popularis* programmes, but Caesar the dictator implemented them with new energy and vision. Augustus, no *popularis*, would follow through almost all Caesar's initiatives when he inherited the same problems along with supreme power.

Where Caesar failed and Augustus succeeded was in dealing with the problem of a politicised army. The state had never taken responsibility for providing for veterans of Rome's wars – more and more of them citizens so poor they had no homes to which they might return after long years of campaigning in Spain or Greece, Africa or Asia Minor. Small wonder that they had come to depend on their generals, and to follow wherever they led. Amazingly Cicero and his allies never tried to tackle this root cause of civil war. Right up to his death, when Cicero was engaged in raising up Octavian as a counterweight to Antony, the only solution the senate attempted was to divide the generals, a solution that traded tyranny for civil strife. When Cicero tried to raise up Octavian against Antony, Brutus reproached him for being willing to create another dictatorship. Cicero complained that the conspirators' plans for what to do after killing Caesar were childish. Both were right. It was left to Augustus to solve the problem by creating a monarchy resting on a standing army, provided for by imperial generosity and fanatically loyal to the Caesars. Neither Cicero nor Brutus would have liked this solution of course.

Yet Julius Caesar at least seemed willing to tackle some of these long-standing issues. And he had other designs too. One was a great war in the east. His departure was set for 18 March: once at the head of a great army he would be unassailable. And there were persistent rumours that he would be crowned king before he left, maybe even on the Ides of March themselves. Plots had been forming slowly: an attack at the games, a mugging on the Sacred Way, even murder during the elections. But they could not be delayed much longer. Time was running out for the conspirators as well as for Caesar.

⧗

The great compromise among the political classes negotiated at such personal cost on 17 and 18 March hardly lasted a week. Veterans, loyal to Caesar and enraged at his murder, drifted into Rome. The populace grumbled. Antony seized the opportunity of Caesar's funeral and the reading out of

Caesar's will (of which every citizen was a beneficiary) to rouse the mob and present himself as Caesar's champion. The conspirators sheltered in their houses again, and were nearly burned alive within them. Brutus spent the rest of this year as urban praetor outside the city, not even daring to return to preside at the Games of Apollo, on which he had spent huge sums already. Cicero left the city too, wandering disconsolately Greecewards but never actually leaving Italy. The letters he and the conspirators exchanged tell a tale of mutual recriminations. Tension grew between Brutus and Cassius.

Meanwhile Octavian advanced steadily on Rome to claim his inheritance. Cicero returned in August to begin a series of rhetorical onslaughts against Antony. Octavian took his place alongside the consuls of 43 and when both conveniently died in battle against Antony's forces he deftly replaced them. But the alliance formed in November 43 between Antony, Lepidus and Octavian was sealed with new proscriptions, new lists of enemies to be slaughtered and robbed with impunity. Cicero's name headed the list. Hunted down, he was killed on 7 December. His head and hands were cut off to be displayed on the rostrum in the forum. Brutus and Cassius lasted a little longer. While the balance of power was being settled in Italy, they moved quickly to the provinces they had been allocated, conducting negotiations at a distance. Throughout 43 and early 42 they moved around the east consolidating their power and wealth with casual acts of brigandage at the expense of their provincial subjects. Antony and Octavian finally came after them in April 42 and the two fatal battles of Philippi were fought in October, not so far from Pharsalus, where both Brutus and Cassius had once fought on Pompey's side against Caesar.

6. The noblest Roman coin of them all? This coin, issued by Brutus, depicts two daggers, the cap that ex-slaves wore to show they had won their freedom, and the (abbreviated) legend 'Ides of March'.

Defeated, both committed suicide. Their deaths cleared the field for new power struggles between Antony, Octavian and Pompey's son Sextus, struggles that took another decade to resolve in Octavian's favour.

⧗

A plot, a murder, chaos and confusion, rumour and recrimination and a failed attempt to put Humpty Dumpty back together again. The ripples of Caesar's assassination spread out through the city, the empire and history.

Those ripples took a while to reach most of the authors on whose testimony depend all modern reconstructions of events. Aside from Cicero's precious correspondence, and some of his philosophical observations, to which I will return in the next chapter, there are almost no contemporary voices. All the same, the first literary echoes of the murder still convey a sense of shock.

About the time that Antony and Octavian were prowling

northern Greece like bloodthirsty wolves, as the suicides of
Brutus and Cassius followed on that of Cato, the historian
Sallust wrote his account of that earlier conspiracy to kill a
consul, the infamous Catilinarian conspiracy of Cicero's consulship in 63 BC. Sallust inserts the affair into a long history
of Roman moral collapse, one in which a competition for
virtue had won the republic an empire, but then that empire
had corrupted the republic with the wealth and leisure it
brought. Rome was raised up by the virtues of her leaders,
then remained for a while strong enough to withstand their
vices, until finally she was unable to produce any leaders
of any virtue whatsoever. Sallust admitted only two excep-
tions:

> … in my own lifetime there appeared two men of out-
> standing virtue, however different they were in charac-
> ter, Marcus Cato and Gaius Caesar. Since the opportunity
> has arisen, I shall not miss the chance to give as good an
> account as I can of the disposition and habits of each.

Both men were now dead, as was Cicero himself. Cato's
suicide 'rather than look upon the face of a tyrant' had
already become a focal point for resistance during Caesar's
dictatorship. More on this anon. Cicero and Brutus had
been among those who had written eulogies of him, and
Caesar had responded with an *Anti-Cato*. The pamphlets
were apparently politely exchanged like the pre-publication
drafts of speeches and philosophical works more regularly
passed around in Cicero's circle. But just four years later we
see Sallust lay his two paragons to rest side by side. Is his
point that morality offers a superior perspective to partisan
politics? Or that their joint example puts all the leaders that

followed to shame? Brutus and Cassius, Antony, Lepidus and Octavian alike? Or does this mark the passing of an age, a sense that one great epoch of republican history was receding rapidly into the past? Sallust's greatest successor, the early-second-century-AD historian Tacitus, would begin his *Annales* with the flourish 'In the beginning Rome had kings' but end that first chapter with the successive dominations of Cinna and Sulla, Pompey and Crassus, Caesar, Antony and Lepidus all swallowed up into the empire of Augustus. 'The Roman republic' has become a mere episode, and liberty a brief intermission in the history of a fundamentally monarchical state. Caesar's death in retrospect seemed not the botched effort to save the republic, but just one chapter in its painfully extended catastrophe.

A second early witness is the poet Virgil, laureate of the first emperor, whose epic *Aeneid* provided imperial Rome with a new myth of origins and a classic that would spellbind Roman schoolchildren until the Fall of Rome to the Goths. His *Georgics* appeared in 29 BC, just a couple of years after the defeat of Antony and Cleopatra at the naval battle of Actium. His *Aeneid* would eventually include a gripping account of the battle. But perhaps it was too soon to sing the miracle in the *Georgics*. At the heart of this mystical poem of agriculture, the cosmos and the human condition lies a set of allegories and apostrophes that sing Octavian as a war-leader, a god and the only hope for war-ravaged Rome and Italy. As the first book draws to a close the poet is showing how heaven has providentially provided weather warnings for the farmer in the passage of the seasons, the waning and waxing of the moon and the appearance of the sun and dusk and dawn.

The sun will give you all these signs. Who would dare
to say the sun misleads? He also often warns us of blind
riots, of conspiracy and tells when wars are insidiously
brewing. He pitied Rome when Caesar was struck down,
covering his brilliant face with sombre gloom, and that
impious age feared eternal night.

Then begins a catalogue of the frightful portents that followed Caesar's death. Mysterious hounds were heard
baying across the sea as well as on dry land, ill-omened
birds were observed, Etna erupted with ferocious flames
and rocks, the sound of weapons echoed across the skies of
Germany and shook the Alps, a great voice called out in the
woods, strange pallid phantoms appeared, animals spoke
in human tongue, rivers dried up, chasms appeared in the
earth, statues of ivory and bronze sweated in their temples
and so on and on. Great floods, springs flowing with blood,
the cries of wolves haunting cities at night, lightning flash-
ing and the blaze of comets. And so to Philippi, and Roman
blood soaking the battlefield. Then, with another shift of
pace and mood, Virgil imagines peaceful farmers plough-
ing that soil in the future, just as instructed in his poem, and
coming across rusty weapons and helmets and great piles
of bones beneath his fields. The Roman cataclysm becomes
mere archaeology, the world's convulsions dwarfed by
the secular turning of the seasons under the plough. The
Georgics forever plays these games with time, harnessing the
cosmic to the pressing needs of the day, and then letting the
immediate take its place against the backdrop of eternity.
But the diversion from Caesar's murder via Philippi to the
great triumphal temple to Caesar Octavianus imagined at
the beginning of Book Three – more or less the dead centre of

the poem – offers a different story to Sallust's great arching sweep of Roman rise and stately fall.

That contrast poses neatly the problem of understanding Caesar's death, the problem of knowing what story it belongs to. Plotting Caesar's murder poses a problem for narrators as well as conspirators. Where the murder falls in the story determines part of its significance. For Virgil, it could be the beginning of a chaos from which Octavian would rescue the state. For Plutarch in his *Life of Caesar* it was naturally the end of the story. But in his *Life of Brutus* it is the defining moment, the existential act that allows Brutus to choose his destiny, including which past he will acknowledge and which future will await him. Appian, like Sallust, fits the murder into a story of collapse: the three books of his *Civil War* begin with the Gracchan crisis and end with Actium. For Suetonius, Caesar's death is again the end of the biography, but Caesar's life is the first of twelve linked biographies. That view of Julius Caesar as the founder of the principate was becoming more and more widely expressed in the second century, as the republic became ancient history.

As the story was retold again and again, Caesar's death became ever more inevitable. The story of the Ides of March is the original Chronicle of a Death Foretold. The portents that in Virgil follow the atrocity came in later versions to precede it as warnings. Plutarch hands the affair over to a Fate that had become unstoppable. He reports strange signs and apparitions, lights in the heavens, great crashing noises across the darkened city and prophetic birds in the forum. The philosopher Strabo, he says, gives an account of a crowd of blazing men charging forward, of a great flame that spontaneously burst from a slave's hand without harming him. Then there are the portents that appeared to Caesar. Magistrates on their way to convene the senate had to perform a sacrifice, so that the internal organs of the animals could be examined for good or bad omens. When Caesar sacrificed on the Ides of March the victim had no heart at all. There is the story of the soothsayer who had warned Caesar about the day, whom Caesar challenged as he went to the senate house saying, 'The Ides of March have come,' to be answered, 'Yes, but they have not yet passed.' The previous night Caesar had dined with Lepidus and when discussion turned to the best ways of dying he expressed a preference for a sudden unexpected death. That night Caesar was woken by all the doors and windows opening suddenly and looked down to see Calpurnia dreaming prophetic nightmares. Plutarch knew two versions, one that she dreamt she was holding his murdered body, the other involving the collapse of their house's monumental ornament. He tells both stories, doubling the effect. Plutarch's readers knew perfectly well what would happen to him. For the narrative, the prophesies increase tension, delaying us, like Caesar, en route to a rendezvous that cannot be avoided. What use Shakespeare made of this is well known. Portents play their part in persuading Brutus to act, bringing about the act itself just as the witches' prophesy leads Macbeth to fulfil it.

Caesar ignored the sacrificial omens, allowed himself to be persuaded to attend the senate despite Calpurnia's entreaties and the prophets' advice, and disregarded the soothsayer. Once at the senate, and despite Brutus's efforts to isolate him, he did receive a letter denouncing the conspiracy ... but never found a chance to read it. For Plutarch greater forces really do seem to be at work. He finds special significance in the statue of Pompey looming over the place of the murder and concludes the *Life of Caesar* with an account of how that great divine power that had watched over Caesar's life exacted revenge on the conspirators. Cassius, after Philippi, killed himself with the same dagger with which he had stabbed Caesar. There was a great comet blazing in the sky for seven days after Caesar's death, the sun was dimmed, and a huge apparition appeared to Brutus on the eve of the last campaign, identifying himself as his evil genius and promising to meet him at Philippi. For Plutarch it was a daemon, one of those lesser divine powers that Platonists believed could intervene in the sub-lunary world. Shakespeare transformed this phantom into Caesar's ghost.

Stories of portents predicting the death of Caesar clearly circulated within a few years of his death. Plutarch harvested a number of sources, but Suetonius, who does tell some of the same stories, has others that Plutarch either did not know or did not choose to tell. One story derives from Cornelius Balbus, a spectacularly rich citizen of Cadiz made a Roman citizen by Pompey, who managed to navigate the complex politics of the sixties and fifties to emerge as one of Caesar's most trusted courtiers. He told how Caesarian colonists at Capua had accidentally disturbed the bones of the city's founder hero and so brought a curse on Caesar. Then there is the story of the horses that Caesar had dedicated to the god Rubicon, which refused their food and began to weep, and that of the royal bird attacked by other birds and dismembered as it flew towards Pompey's senate house, and a dream that Caesar had of flying up to join Jupiter.

Stories like this gave meaning to Caesar's death, confirmed its cosmic significance and imbued the story of his life with a special value. Most of all they gave it shape, an end worthy of its beginning, a sense that its conclusion followed naturally from what had gone before. Tales of the operation of fate in a sense also exonerated both Caesar and his murderers from responsibility. And they offered reassurance that the murder was not simply a botched coup, an ill-thought-out act of petty rivalry, a pointless waste that changed nothing, or else that changed things only for the worse.

⧗

The historically minded might want an explanation for Caesar's death. Our ancient witnesses compete to offer reasons for his murder. As usual there are two levels of argument, the overt one over the most important cause or causes and the unstated dispute over what constitutes an appropriate explanation for a cataclysm of this kind. So Plutarch, moralist as well as biographer, must find in the history of events the collision of individuals, each propelled by the logic of their characters and their choices, even when those choices are constrained by greater powers. Caesar must die because of the way Caesar chose to live. Brutus must kill him because he is Brutus. Historians face the opposite difficulty, that the grand narrative of the fall of the republic threatens to render trivial the details of Caesar's conduct during his brief dictatorship. Yet the proximate causes for Caesar's murder must be found in the three and a half years between the defeat of Pompey at Pharsalus on 9 August 48 BC and the Ides of March of 44 BC.

Resistance to Caesar did not crumble immediately after the battle. Pompey himself survived until the end of September, when he was murdered by the Egyptians, apparently in an attempt to win Caesar's friendship. Caesar spent much of the next two years reasserting his control over the armies and provinces scattered around the Mediterranean. Caesar moved from Egypt back through Syria and Asia, was back in Italy in late 47 to settle a mutiny, but by the end of the year had left to face the Pompeian army in north Africa, now rallied by Cato who had gone to join them at around the same time as Brutus had defected to Caesar. That army was defeated at the battle of Thapsus, and Cato committed suicide in April of 46. Caesar returned to Rome to celebrate a series of triumphs in September and October. But Pompey's eldest son Gnaeus survived until defeated at the last battle of the civil war at Munda in Spain in 45. He was captured and executed: so much for Caesar's claim that he would have spared Pompey had he taken him alive. Pompey's younger son, Sextus, remained at liberty at the time of Caesar's death. The hectic shuttling between the provinces and Italy shows not just his trademark *celeritas Caesaris* – Caesarian speed – but also the shaky grip he retained on power. Pharsalus, in other words, was no Actium. Yet although Sextus Pompey remained at liberty, Caesar faced no real opposition in the provinces in 44 BC, nor is there any sign of hostility in Italy or among the Roman people.

Caesar died because he failed to win, or to retain, the loyalty of that inner circle of the Roman elite, for all that he spared their lives, gave them magistracies and promised them rich provinces. Certainly he might have taken other precautions. Taking better notice of soothsayers would have been the least of these. He might have murdered his enemies after Pompey's death, or he might have resigned the dictatorship. Sulla did both. He might have surrounded himself with a bodyguard. This is what his imperial successors would do. Or he might have left Rome once again and dominated it from the provinces, as Pompey had done and many emperors would again. Caesar was indeed preparing new wars at the time of his murder. Evasion or solution?

Caesar once said that Sulla's decision to resign the dictatorship showed that he was ignorant of the first rules of statesmanship. Thoughtful and sensitive to the mistakes of his predecessors, Caesar made his own. The crucial period was the final twelve months. By March 45 only Rome remained to be won. Caesar took his time in confronting this last challenge. He lingered in Spain, marched back slowly through southern France, founding colonies, adjusting civic statuses, fine-tuning the apparatus of provincial government. By the time he arrived in northern Italy it was midsummer. The Roman Senate and the courts were always in recess during the hottest period of the Mediterranean year. Many aristocrats – like medieval popes after them – left the city for rural retreats, in the Alban lakes, at Tivoli or in the Sabine hills. So there was no cause to hurry back, and Caesar did not in fact return until October.

He entered the city in a triumph. Over the next few months he was phenomenally energetic advancing the public works he had begun in 46. These included remodelling the Campus Martius and the end of the forum closest to the Capitol. A library was planned, a great theatre, and more mundane but essential constructions: road building, harbour installations, drainage schemes. The calendar was revised, and with it the sacred rites of the city ordered and restored. Meanwhile the senate struggled to devise appropriate honours. Caesar's birthday and the day of his victory at Munda were made holidays, there were statues, he was hailed and given the title *Father of the Fatherland*, honours normally paid only to gods. Caesar's party and the senate both seemed engaged in searching to find him an appropriate role, but there were no good precedents to follow, and each side gave casual offence. A tribune failed to stand for Caesar as he was carried past in his triumphal procession in October: Caesar behaved high-handedly at the elections in December when he appointed a surrogate consul to stand in for one who had died a day before his office expired. Incidents like these multiplied, and Caesar's imminent departure on campaign set a deadline on finding some more permanent solution. Finally, in early February, Caesar accepted the title of Dictator for Life. Just over a month later he was dead.

2

TALKING TYRANNICIDE

Assassination is always a serious business, and one unfamiliar to most of us. Most readers of this book probably live in liberal democracies. This broad and vague category is not without its ideological significance. The political theorist Francis Fukuyama notoriously argued in 1989 that liberal democracy – a combination of free market economics and a politics based on citizenship and constitutionality – was not only the dominant political ideology today but had also brought about the End of History. By this he meant that our kind of civil society had out-competed communism, fascism and more traditional forms of government, was a system free of fundamental internal contradictions and so was the end point of mankind's political evolution. Although not yet installed in a perfected form throughout the globe, liberal democracy was an ideal that could not be improved on. Resistance movements, including fundamentalisms of all kinds, were merely growing pains most evident in those parts of the world undergoing the most rapid modernisation. Even at the time, some of this thesis seemed complacent in the extreme.

Liberal democracy and its limits set the terms for all modern considerations of assassination. For those of us lucky enough to live in civil societies, political murder is

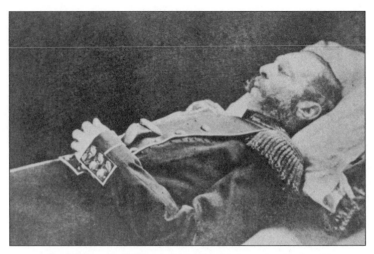

7. *Tsar Alexander II lying in state after his assassination in 1881.*

very unusual, and when it occurs it feels like an assault on the moral foundations of the state. Why is this? One reason is that liberal states claim not only a monopoly of legitimate violence, but also exclude violence from the everyday experience of their citizens, and themselves employ lethal violence only rationally and when absolutely necessary. So in most states only soldiers and police officers operating under tightly defined terms of engagement are permitted to kill. Judicial violence has been progressively reduced and concealed. Michel Foucault showed how the great festivals of torture and execution that were used in absolutist Europe to punish the most notorious villains – regicides among them – were suppressed around the turn of the eighteenth and nineteenth centuries in favour of less visible executions, and of incarceration. Most liberal democracies – the United States is the main exception – have abandoned judicial killing.

Violence in politics is one of the most common signs taken to show that a state does not live up to the ideals of liberal democracy. What makes a country a dictatorship is a liability to military coups, show-trials, summary executions and death squads, and the regular use of torture and the abuse of human rights. Technically the absence of multi-party elections, the existence of censorship or even excessive government intervention in the market would disqualify countries from Fukuyama's category. But violence is the touchstone. It is when states seem unable to control violence or abuse it themselves that liberal democracy is held to be failing, or perhaps not yet fully realised. The metaphor of 'maturity' is often employed, as if violence is a mark of political youth, or adolescence. In a triumph of hope over experience, we still imagine all states groping towards civil society. The terrifying lessons of fascism and Stalinism have not completely dented our faith in the gradual emergence of a rational world order.

Have we in the West really outgrown all this? Certainly in the past European states were less ambitious where violence was concerned, and left the imposition of order to local lords and communities, and above all to the heads of families. But was this world not swept away in the French and American revolutions? The Roman republic was one of the main political models for both French and American revolutionaries, but they were, thank goodness, extremely selective in their borrowings from Rome. The idea of human rights is unthinkable in antiquity, for all that Stoic philosophy taught some sort of brotherhood of all human beings. Ancient rights derived from the state, and occasionally from inter-state diplomacy. The Roman concept of a Law of Nations was a pale forerunner of our ideals of universal human rights. Civil rights were transformed, from the classical model that allocated different kinds of trial and penalty on the basis of political rank, to a non-negotiable package of rights for each citizen. Enlightenment values, and some Christian ones, set a new direction. Not that slavery, child labour or a tacit agreement that 'domestic violence' was not a matter for public authorities disappeared immediately. But the logic of the political and social forces set loose in the eighteenth century has been to establish a new economy of violence. Those who criticise instances of the abuse of power and neglect of rights by particular liberal democracies almost always argue for more progress in this direction. One reason that Sharia, the strict rule of Islamic law, terrifies so many in the West is that the violent punishments it imposes for some crimes seem, in the light of our own history, to be a retrograde movement, to threaten to turn the clock back. Bad history as that might be, the experiences of Nigeria, Iran and Saudi Arabia all suggest that despite its spiritually elevated aspirations Sharia has the potential to bring back into view some kinds of violence that had been absent from the West for a couple of centuries, among them judicial stonings and amputations and perhaps even family courts with the power to exercise the death penalty over their members.

Liberal democracy is far from perfect and it certainly serves some classes better than others. For much of the early twentieth century many left-leaning intellectuals searched in vain for an alternative route. But Soviet communism was, in Richard Crossman's ringing phrase, the God that Failed: it was so hard to find any socialist utopia without its Gulags. Today we are more conscious than ever of the scant respect for the rights of women and children in most non-western societies. But it is not only on those grounds that we condemn the alternatives to liberal democracy. Violence once again enters the equation. Of all these 'other' states, we reserve our harshest condemnation not for those that fail their own people, like Sudan, or for those which stifle political debate, like Burma, or which do both, like Zimbabwe, but for the so-called pariah-nations that sponsor terrorism. We fear contagion, the leakage of their irrational violence into our well-ordered societies.

But there are at least two reasons why it is wrong to see the world of liberal democracy as an embattled refuge from violence. First, liberal democracies are deeply implicated in the violence that dogs many other states. Indirectly, the success of capitalist market economies has contributed to the impoverishment of many of the parts of the world where liberal states repeatedly fail, and in others the collapse of imperial systems has created conditions in which democracy found it hard to take root. There is, after all, a grim geography of political violence today, and it is not a geography of distance from liberalism and democracy. The military dictatorships of the Far East and parts of Latin America; the poorest post-colonial successor states of the British, French, Belgian and Soviet empires; communist China and North Korea and some parts of the Arab world: in all these regions western governments have been too involved, not too far removed. Directly, the operation of the arms trade, the Cold War militarisation of other societies, the deliberate destabilisation of some regimes and western support for some despotic governments have combined to create conditions in which terrorism thrives. The notion of the autonomy of sovereign nations, a key tenet of liberal democratic thought, provides a convenient pretext for non-intervention. None of this excuses political murder, but it gives some reason to see these states not as under-developed democracies so much as part of a global division of violence.

The second reason not to regard political violence as a sign of underdevelopment is that modern terrorism, in its strict sense, came into existence at the same moment as the liberal nation-state. The French Revolution and the Reconstruction of the Union after the American Civil War were bathed in it. It flourished across late-nineteenth-century Europe when new political ideas and the invention of dynamite formed a lethal cocktail. The spread of parliamentary democracy and civil society around the globe brought terrorism and assassination with it. The very claim to manage and monopolise violence challenges the dissident to refute it. The same mass media that made modern nationalisms and modern states possible has provided terrorists with the promise that their atrocities would have the maximum possible impact. Terror is powerful in civilised societies because it challenges our claim to manage violence and to remove it from the everyday experience of our citizens. And of all kinds of terror, political assassination – the public murder of the most prominent leaders – is both the most difficult to achieve, and the most shocking when it succeeds.

Republican Rome was in most respects quite unlike the modern states we inhabit. It was a violent, under-policed, volatile world with little social justice and few restraints on the whims of the rich. But political assassinations planned in cold blood – as opposed to killings and suicides in the heat of civil war, or lynchings that took place during panicky riots – were just as infrequent as they are in our societies. The reason is easy to discern. No group in Rome was more committed to the rule of law than the propertied classes, whose interests law largely served. Quite apart from that,

the rulers of the world inhabited a marble village, surrounded by neighbours, friends, relatives and rivals they
had known since childhood. What could possess them to let
loose the fratricidal force of political murder in that community? What considerations could have induced so many of
them not only to sanction political murder, but to perpetrate
it with their own hands?

Yet they did let it loose, and were able to persuade
themselves at least that they did so for noble, and principled reasons. Uncovering the intellectual and moral roots
of tyrannicide will take us from the philosophy and oratory
of the conquered Greek world that Cicero and his peers so
coveted, back to the dawn of both Greek and Roman histories. But lest we judge them too harshly, let us begin with the
contemporary ethical case for political murder, as formulated
against and within our own pacific and civilised world.

Four US presidents have been assassinated between the
murder of Abraham Lincoln in 1865 and that of John F.
Kennedy in 1963. Two prime ministers of India have been
assassinated, Indira Gandhi in 1984 and her son Rajiv Gandhi
in 1991, the latter two years after he had left office. Only
one British prime minister has been assassinated, Spencer
Perceval, shot at the entrance of the House of Commons in
1812. But successful political murders of heads of government are only the tip of the iceberg. Assassination attempts
failed against the following American US presidents: Andrew
Jackson, Theodore Roosevelt, Harry S. Truman, Gerald Ford,
Ronald Reagan, Bill Clinton and George W. Bush, and
against the British prime ministers Margaret Thatcher and

8. This drawing shows the assassination of President McKinley in 1901 at the Pan-American Exposition. The President is shown dignified and calm in front of an American flag. His assassin, Leon Czolgosz, was apparently inspired by the anarchist assassination of King Umberto I of Italy the previous year.

John Major, to say nothing of earlier plots against Parliament itself. A much longer list could be compiled if candidates for office and other senior politicians were to be included. The assassinations of Mahatma Gandhi in 1948, of Malcolm X in 1965 and of Martin Luther King in 1968 and the attempt on the life of Pope John Paul II in 1981 all had plausible political motivations. When is an assassination just a murder, and when is it political? These are difficult lines to draw. The attempt made on Ronald Reagan's life in 1981 was committed by a man deeply involved in extremist politics but also apparently obsessed with the actress Jodie Foster, whom he hoped to impress by the killing. How different is this from the murder of John Lennon in Central Park by an obsessed fan just three months before? At least some attempts to murder prominent politicians have been motivated not so much by a desire to derail a political programme or punish a political opponent, as to capitalise on the celebrity status of the victim. Motivations are not easily dissociated in practice. Indira Gandhi died because of her past hard-line attitude to would-be separatists, because her death would undoubtedly weaken the Congress Party, and because she stood for a political dynasty and a vision of a united federal India that appalled and frightened many. Perhaps a better way of putting this is to admit the irrational element in many attempted and successful political murders. Presidents and prime ministers today, like the czars, kings and archdukes they replaced, embody the nations they rule or reign over. Their human vulnerability – like that of the innocent victims of terrorist mass killings – makes them proxy-targets for the incorporeal and much more powerful apparatus of the state.

Assassination has had a powerful attraction for writers of fiction. Terrorist plots have been a key component of the modern novel at least since Conrad's *Secret Agent* was first published in 1907, a novelisation of an actual anarchist bomb attack on the Royal Greenwich Observatory in 1894. Unlike many modern treatments, *The Secret Agent* tried to get into the psychology of the terrorist, to expose his tragedy as well as the roots of what Conrad in an author's note written in 1920 called the 'absurd cruelty' of the actual explosion. The absurdity of terrorist murder made it a source of fascination for existentialists. Sartre considered it in his drama *Les Mains Sales*, which explores the muddled psychology of a reluc-

9. The assassination of Spencer Perceval by the Liverpool businessman John Bellingham who blamed the government for his debts. The only Prime Minister to have been assassinated, Perceval's interests are listed on the official 10, Downing Street website as 'Playing games with his children' and 'the study of Biblical prophecy'.

tant but ultimately successful assassin in a post-war Balkan state. Personal and principled motives are entangled as the troubled protagonist tries to find his way to an authentic act that would prove and define himself. Geoffrey Household's classic thriller *Rogue Male* tells the tale of a wealthy and civilised British gentleman who crosses from Poland into a neighbouring country and attempts to assassinate a foreign head of state. His motives are obscure even to him, a mixture of patrician distaste for a vulgar and sordid regime and a personal quest to avenge a loved one. Captured and tortured, he nevertheless manages to escape to England where he is hunted down by British sympathisers of the foreign power, but he outwits them through a mixture of masculine courage and resourcefulness and sets off back overseas to finish the job he started. The novel was published in 1939, and Household left the identity of the target obscure, allegedly because he was unsure when writing whether Britain was about to ally with Hitler against Stalin or the reverse. Assassination has more than once been a convenient place in which to explore the relations between individual and state, the limits of moral freedom and state power, and the conditions in which murder for political ends might be justified in civil society. *The Day of the Jackal*, chronicling a fictional attack on General de Gaulle, pits an enormously powerful state against an unimaginably resourceful assassin. Killer, target and the power of the security forces are all romanticised in the struggle to commit, or prevent, the ultimate crime. The real De Gaulle is said to have survived thirty-one assassination attempts.

Perhaps no fictional figure epitomises the tangled relations between civility and political murder better than does James Bond. Urbane and civilised, a former officer and a perpetual gentleman, he moves easily in establishment circles and exclusive social venues, a hyper-masculine hero whose savoir-faire is never defeated. But he also possesses that most exclusive sanction in a democratic society, a licence to kill. In defence of all the values we most treasure, he is permitted to break our greatest taboo, to commit premeditated murder for queen and country. Interestingly, in successive films, the debonair and elegant Bond has supplanted the sometimes sentimental, but often ruthless protagonist of Ian Fleming's novels. Despite Timothy Dalton's attempt to harden the image, wisecracks (hardly present in the novels) have replaced violence, and the killings have become schematic and cartoon-like. Movie-Bond still has no scruples about killing, but the plot is often engineered to allow him to do so in self-defence, and at little personal cost. The grim mechanics of the assassin's trade are now concealed by his smooth exterior, while the marked violence towards women and fascination with torture – perhaps Fleming's most personal contribution to the novels – are reduced to a minimum. But the extreme restraint of Her Majesty's Secret Service is still expressed in Bond's number, 007. He has few peers. We kill sparingly.

Or do we? For debates over the ethics of assassination continue in the corridors of power even in the liberal West. These are best documented within the United States, partly because of the admirable openness of American politics compared to that of many European governments. During 1975 a Senate Select Committee on Intelligence chaired by senator Frank Church reviewed the activities of the CIA in this respect. It revealed involvements in a number of assassination attempts against foreign leaders during the height of the Cold War. Most of them were unsuccessful, some farcically so. Fidel Castro of Cuba, Rafael Trujillo of the Dominican Republic, Abdul Karim Qassem of Iraq and Patrice Lumumba of the Congo were among the targets. The last case at least was ordered by the White House. Other leaders died in CIA-backed coups or were killed by the Agency's local allies. Assassination attempts of this kind were largely renounced after the Church committee's report, whether because of public protest at the principle and the company the CIA were shown to keep … or because of their low success rate. President Reagan issued an executive order in 1981 banning any US government employee or representative from engaging in assassination. But it was the same president who, five years later, with support from the British prime minister Margaret Thatcher, authorised an air strike on the barracks in Tripoli where General Qaddafi normally slept. In the event they did not succeed in killing Qaddafi but killed his fifteen-month-old daughter and two of his adopted sons.

More recent assassination attempts have taken the form of targeting missiles on the suspected locations of enemy leaders such as Osama bin Laden and Saddam Hussein. The US is of course not the only democracy to have engaged in assassination and similar activities: it is just one of the more transparent. Successive Israeli governments have regarded the extra-judicial killing of terrorist leaders as legitimate and necessary. The French government sponsored and colluded in a number of assassinations in the course of the Algerian war of 1954–62. Allegations of involvement by British security forces in the killing of Republican Irish terrorists and perhaps of their supporters remain the subject of enquiries and controversy. The term assassination has been avoided in recent statements about the permissibility of the use of lethal force against terrorists. Terms such as 'the War on Terror' and 'Regime Change' and 'Shoot to Kill Policies' partly serve to muddy the legal status of actions that might result in the death of enemy leaders. John Major's announcement that he did not seek Saddam Hussein's death, but that if his death was a result of hostilities he 'would not weep', obscures the seriousness of what is being debated.

So our own political leaders – despite the vast differences between our world and antiquity – find themselves in ethical dilemmas over assassination similar to those faced by Brutus and his conspirators. The most decent of them struggle to preserve a society in which civil rights are protected for the many, by compromising the rights of the few. Nor are these ethics limited to the corridors of power. Action movies, cop shows and detective novels repeatedly offer us rule-breaking heroes whose 'unorthodox' and sometimes brutal methods succeed against villains of unquestionable guilt. Their superior officers, office-bound and ineffectual, protest in vain. But from Marlowe to Rebus our sympathies are directed to maimed heroes, pariah paladins whose personal commitments to justice are stereotypically paired with an inability to participate fully in the society they guard, marked most of all by their romantic and domestic inadequacies. This contemporary ethic of heroism is insidious. It empowers a rhetoric that sweeps civil liberties aside. It justifies the inexcusable.

Assassination has always been used sparingly by civil societies. It is, after all, murder, and no government wishes to convey the opinion that this is more than exceptionally legitimate. Yet faced with certain kinds of threats that seem to admit no other solution, removing a key enemy by any means possible has had its attractions. During the Cold War the incentive was the fantasy that the Cuban revolution or the spread of Soviet-friendly regimes in South America, Africa or Eastern Asia could be stopped if just a few key individuals were removed. Today the motivation is to remove a key dictator or a terrorist mastermind. Liberal governments try to balance the guilt incurred by one act of dubious morality against the possible good of the greater number. But this is not merely principled utilitarianism. Distance sanitises. Killing a European leader or a political opponent in the US would seem a much greater crime than eliminating the ruler of a different kind of state. Classifying terrorists as enemy combatants or Middle Eastern presidents as despots puts them conveniently beyond the moral pale. The language of wartime evokes the spectre of temporary and extraordinary licence. These are unusual times, we don't normally behave this way, desperate situations call for desperate measures. We don't kill people like us, and so it is important that their difference be recognised. Perhaps this reassures those who give the orders more than it does any member of the public who might discover what has been done in our name.

⌛

When the Roman senate – battered by Caesar's murder and its threat of wholesale carnage – met in the temple of Tellus on 17 March 44 BC, reconciliation had already been agreed on. All the same it was important, for form's sake, that something appropriate be said, that some semblance of a debate should confirm the behind-the-scenes deals. Cicero, in his role as elder statesman, did the honours. In his speech he reminded his audience of an event in ancient Greek history, when a botched attempt at overthrowing the Athenian democracy had failed but was followed by a general amnesty rather than retaliation. The sentiment suited the crisis in Rome, but it was an inexact parallel.

The greatest thinkers of classical Athens worried more about the despotism exercised by the masses over the wealthy, or by imperial cities over other Greek communities, than about tyranny and its remedies. Politics meant, for most, what it meant for Plato and Aristotle among philosophers and for Demosthenes and Aeschines among orators: *ta politika*, the life of the city state, the *polis*. Political thought was a quest for the best constitution, one that would establish the proper balance of power between rich and poor, the limits of citizenship, the respective role of assemblies, councils, magistrates and law-courts. Statesmanship meant mastering rhetoric, the art of persuasion, and learning how best to advise, warn, chastise and flatter assemblies, armies and juries. Kings were remembered from Homer, and traditions persisted about the spectacular and terrible tyrants of the archaic age. Kings and tyrants still existed in classical times on the margins of the Greek world, in Sicily and Italy for example, in Cyrenaica and the Crimea. A few members of Athens's alienated aristocracy – among them many of the wealthy youths that gathered around Socrates – were attracted and fascinated by the possibilities of monarchy. Xenophon idolised the Spartan monarch Agesilaos, wrote an account of the education of the Persian King Cyrus and a treatise on King Hieron of Syracuse. Plato argued that a state should be ruled only by those wise enough to rule well, and imagined a philosopher king the best of possible rulers. His contemporary Isocrates wrote letters of advice to several autocrats. Absolute power wielded by a wise man seemed so much superior to the patent failures and idiocies of democracy. A few Athenian intellectuals, among them Euripides and Aristotle, even spent time in the Macedonian royal court. But it was not until Alexander captured the Persian empire that Greek intellectuals turned their full attention from civic politics to the theorisation of monarchy.

Alexander's death left his empire divided into a series of mighty and petty kingdoms that stretched from the Adriatic to the Hindu Kush and from southern Russia to the cataracts of the Nile. These were no national states, and their boundaries were always fluid. Most kingdoms consisted simply of the land that a given king and his army could dominate. Court intrigues were inevitable, and any king who lost the support of his hereditary army was finished. Conversely new kingdoms could be created overnight by enterprising generals, while others shrank to tiny rumps if their dynasties threw up weak heirs. This new and chaotic world is conventionally termed Hellenistic, and this was the Greek world that the Romans conquered. By the time Sulla, Pompey and Caesar began their careers, the greatest Hellenistic monarchies had, in fact, already been pulverised by Roman arms. Yet Mithridates, King of Pontus, and Cleopatra, Queen of Egypt, along with a cast of second-division petty monarchs, still offered Roman generals beguiling visions of splendid autocracy. Rumour had it that Tiberius Gracchus, the popular tribune slaughtered by a mob of senators in 133 BC, had been offered a golden crown by his Greek friends. Pompey was treated like a king as he processed through Eastern cities. Caesar was offered a crown by Antony during the festival of the Lupercalia, exactly one month before his assassination. He refused it, but many felt he was trying it on for size. And every Roman grandee of the last generation of the republic was fascinated by Alexander the Great. Alexander stood for a style of kingship that had, by Caesar's day, acquired a rather precise definition. That definition was largely the creation of Greek intellectuals in city states which had long ago lost their autonomy, their democracy and their liberty. The theory of monarchy they devised was the ultimate origin of medieval and renaissance Mirrors of Princes. It idealised monarchs that ruled absolutely, but enlightened with magnanimous regard for their subjects, especially the Greek ones and those with property. These kings they distinguished sharply from tyrants, building a moral edifice on Aristotle's rather dry taxonomy of autocrats. They learned new means of persuading kings as opposed to the masses, adjusting the tropes of flattery. These kings were treated almost as gods – while they ruled. But they were also reminded of the fate that awaited tyrants – murder and then posthumous execration. Meanwhile in Rome, as some generals raised their heads so high above their peers that they seemed like kings, these Greek tracts were read and pondered. This was an age of philosopher senators, and in the run-up to the Ides of March they well understood the crucial question to be posed. What kind of autocrat was Caesar? King or tyrant?

⧗

Cicero was not part of the original conspiracy, even if Brutus did cry out his name after stabbing Caesar. But it is Cicero who offers the fullest reflection on the ethics of Caesar's murder. It occurs in *On Duties*, his last philosophical work, written in the autumn of 44 BC, about six months after Caesar's death and just over a year before his own.

In the introduction to the second book *On Duties*, Cicero defends himself against the charge that writing philosophy is a waste of his efforts.

As long as the state was ruled by those to which it had entrusted itself, I devoted to it the whole of my energy and attention. Now everything has fallen under the domination of a single man, and there is no longer any place for my advice or authority. Most of all, I have lost those great men who were my allies in protecting the state. But I have not surrendered myself to grief, which might have overwhelmed me if I had not resisted it fiercely, nor have I retreated to a life of pleasure unworthy of an educated man.

Cicero's philosophy was no retreat from his political concerns. The unifying theme of the remarkable volume of writing he produced in the last three years of his life was the application of philosophy – almost all of it Greek in origin – to the pragmatic concerns of a Roman aristocrat. Addressed to his son, *On Duties* more generally marks out the next generation of Roman aristocrats as those in need of moral guidance. If there were to be no more opportunities to hear Cicero speak, let them at least read him. And read him they did. Cicero's works became classics almost at once, and remained the basis of Roman education for centuries. St Augustine claimed that he was inspired to study philosophy by Cicero's manifesto the *Hortensius*.

On Duties was Cicero's contribution to a long-running set of debates over the relationship of what was honourable or virtuous to what was expedient or useful. The dilemma is a timeless one. Most of us believe that some actions are more virtuous than others. Cicero's list of virtues in Book 1 includes Justice and Liberality (aspects of Social Justice); Greatness of Spirit and Decency, and he discusses these in the first book. Most of us also believe that we should bear in mind the likely consequences of alternative courses of action when we choose between them. For Cicero, ever the politician, the most desired consequence, discussed in Book 2, was to win the support and esteem of other good men. The key ethical dilemma, faced in Book 3, was how to balance a decision based on the virtue of a course of action against one based on its consequences. Assassination poses the problem acutely. Murder is among the most serious of misdeeds, but are there not circumstances when the good that comes out of killing a tyrant is so great that the crime is justified by the results? This problem has not gone away.

Sadly, Cicero's answer will not satisfy many of us. He argued that the benefits of wrong-doing are only *apparent* benefits, and that there are therefore never any genuine conflicts between what is virtuous and what is useful. This depends on some philosophical sleight of hand. He appeals to the Stoic idea that all humans form a fellowship and so actions need to be judged by their consequences for all humankind, rather than for the actor alone. Selfish advantage is thus no real advantage if won at the expense of others. If only things were so simple! Elsewhere, Cicero and his contemporary Sallust indulged in a familiar Roman form of nostalgia, imagining how perfectly civil society functioned in days gone by, when competition between great men benefited the state, when laws and the prerogatives of class were respected, and deference was paid to the mighty by their inferiors. Cicero's own life was lived in 'interesting times'. More than ever before, now, individuals pursued what was useful to themselves rather than what was virtuous or useful to mankind as a whole.

Caesar's murder haunts *On Duties*. Cicero's private letters of the time express quite candidly his disappointment in Brutus and Cassius. The murder was a noble act, but they seemed not to have thought what to do next, and the rise of Antony appalled Cicero. But a philosophical treatise was not the place to dwell on missed opportunities. Instead Cicero drew lessons. Consider these words on moral dangers faced by the greatest of men:

But most people, as soon as the desire for military commands, magistracies and glory seizes them, forget all about justice. As Ennius says:

'With kingship no contract is sacred nor is there any trust'.

The truth of this is plain to see. For whenever the situation means that only one person can be pre-eminent, competition becomes so intense that indeed it is very difficult to keep any bond sacred. The recent insolence of Gaius Caesar made this very clear, when he ran roughshod over all laws human and divine to win that supremacy which he had persuaded himself in error should be his. The worst thing about this situation is that the desire for office, command, power and glory seems to arise most strongly in the greatest souls and the most brilliant intellects. So we should be all the more careful not to err in that direction.

The figure of Caesar as a man of exceptional talent, whose greatness leads him to crime and disaster, has obvious appeal. It admits Caesar's greatness but makes it a cause, rather than a contradiction, of his villainy. It even makes some sort of apologetic sense of the honours pragmatically paid both to him, and to his murderers, in the immediate aftermath of the Ides of March. And it establishes Caesar clearly as a prototype not to be imitated. Antony, Octavian, Lepidus and whoever else comes next, please take note! Cicero pointedly returns later in the book to those whose greatness of spirit makes them long for sole power, and ignore considerations of fairness, argument or even the law. Caesar makes other casual appearances, mostly to point out deficiencies in virtue.

Inevitably, Caesar is bracketed with that other dictator, Sulla. The tyrant conventionally – according to the conventions of the Greeks, that is – had respect for neither persons nor property. Cicero attacks both Roman dictators for confiscating property from its rightful owners and for giving it to others. Caesar was, in Cicero's view, even more blameworthy than Sulla since his redistributions were ideologically driven. Like all popular politicians, Caesar had promoted redistributions of land, generally from rich to poor. Cicero regarded schemes of this kind as an attack on the very foundations of civil society. As ever there were Greek precedents, and Cicero lists them. Closely linked with land distribution in classical thought were proposals for debt relief (another assault on property). A desire for the abolition of debts was claimed as one cause of Catiline's conspiracy. Caesar as dictator had succeeded where Catiline had failed – Cicero claimed – for he abolished arrears of interest in 49 BC. But it is on Caesar's eminence rather than on his policies that Cicero focuses in his most explicit statements about tyrannicide. Here he found a limit to that community of interest among all humans on which he based his arguments for the identity of the honourable and the expedient.

> We have no fellowship with tyrants. Indeed we are utterly estranged from them. It is not against nature to steal, if you can, from a man whom it would be virtuous to kill. The entire pestilential and impious race should be exterminated from the community of mankind.

Like diseased limbs that imperil the survival of the body, Cicero continues, tyrants should be amputated. This then, is Cicero's resolution of the ethical dilemma posed by assassination. One crime removes a man – even the most talented man and even one to whom personal debts of gratitude are owed – from the moral universe: that crime is tyranny. All that remains, then, is to determine who the tyrants are.

Was Caesar a tyrant? Cicero refers to Caesar as a tyrant repeatedly in his correspondence with his confidant Atticus. But had Caesar's desire for power really been so much greater than that of his rivals? Cicero invoked Cato's heroic death as a proof of tyranny. But this was a poor argument. Cicero reserves full discussion of tyranny for Book 2 of *On Duties*. Cicero argues for the importance of human solidarity, of common effort and endeavour. Agriculture, civilisation, all the arts and technologies that civilisation brings are the product of human fellowship. The greatest benefit that virtue can win is the support of others. This line of thought brings him to leadership, and to the good and bad reasons for which humans submit to it. Some lead by inspiring fear and hatred, others by inspiring love. Which method was most powerful Caesar's career had illustrated.

> It was not appreciated before that no power can withstand the hatred of many, but it has recently become well known. For it is not just the death of this tyrant, whose rule the state was compelled to endure by military might, and whom it obeys even now he is dead, that shows how powerful the hatred of men can be. The similar deaths of the rest of the tyrants, virtually none of whom escaped this fate, tells the same story.

Fear is a poor guardian of a regime, when compared to love. Suppressing freedom only makes it fight back harder. Having inserted Caesar into the category of tyrants, Cicero summons up a supporting cast of examples who lived in fear of their subjects. Dionysius, tyrant of Sicilian Syracuse, would not let his barber use a naked blade and had his hair singed instead. Alexander, tyrant of Thessalian Pherae, never slept with his wife without taking an armed bodyguard with him. The tyrant's fear is justified. Alexander was indeed murdered by his wife, another Sicilian tyrant, Phalaris, by the whole population of Agrigento, and so on.

It is the recent history of Rome that ushers in Cicero's final denunciation of Caesar. Towards the end of the third book he considers objections to his argument, including the perennial question of whether there might be circumstances in which normal ethical rules do not apply. Cicero asks whether there is no object so valuable or so advantageous that it would be worth acting dishonourably to obtain. No, he responds, forcefully. To accept that would make you no better than Pompey. (Cicero has already dealt with Marius a few chapters earlier.) Pompey's crime was to ally with Caesar for his own advantage and against the interests of the state. Caesar used to quote a line of Euripides's *Phoenician Women*: 'If the law is to be broken, then let it be broken for the sake of ruling.' The speaker in the play was one of two brothers whose rivalry for control of the city of Thebes was the theme of a great Greek mythic cycle about civil war. Caesar deserved his death, concludes Cicero, because he made an exception of the one crime that is most criminal of all. Caesar desired to become king of Rome and master of the world. That put him on a level with parricides. Caesar did such damage to himself by these acts that his life was no longer any real benefit to him, and so his murder should bring gratitude as well as glory.

Caesar was not the only republican statesman to be accused of tyranny. Indeed he was not the first to attract the charge.

Cicero's condemnation in *On Duties* was no retrospective justification of his murder. Perhaps it was the first careful working out of these ideas, and it was certainly influential for later theorisers of regicide and tyrannicide. But there is good evidence that some Romans had already absorbed some sense of tyranny, and of its remedies, well before the dictatorship of Caesar. And these ideas were available to Brutus and Cassius as they struggled to find a way out of Rome's political stalemate in the run-up to the Ides of March.

A few years later, the historian Sallust – another senator forced into retirement – wrote his *Histories* of the decade or so that had followed the dictatorship of Sulla. Early in the work the Roman consul Lepidus accuses Sulla of tyranny. Sulla's tyranny is characterised by crimes and treachery, cruelty and arbitrary action, but is represented chiefly as the suppression of freedom and subversion of the laws. Lepidus savages the aristocratic supporters of the tyrant – Bruti, Aemilii, Lutatii. Sulla is cruel, he has no shame and he will never surrender his power.

> So there is no longer any opportunity for rest or that dignified retirement from public affairs, of the kind which many honest men used to seek. Now you must command or you must be enslaved. If you do not inspire fear, Romans, you must be subject to it. What else remains? What human or divine laws have not been polluted. The Roman People, that recently governed nations, has been deprived of its mastery, its glory, its laws and has been stripped of its livelihood and its respect. Not even the rations of slaves have been left to it.

Lepidus goes on to speak of Sulla's confiscations of property, his murder of innocent men, his harshness to the Roman people. Did Sulla's opponents really speak this way? Or has Sallust reinterpreted the dictatorship of Sulla in terms borrowed from the dictatorship of Caesar? Making Sulla the *real* tyrant, perhaps? Sallust had himself been a Caesarian in the civil wars of the forties.

There is a more surprising precedent in some of Cicero's earliest speeches, those that had first made his reputation as an orator. Cicero's *Verrines* were composed in 70 BC, a decade after Sulla's dictatorship, and their target, Gaius Verres, a former governor of Sicily on trial for maladministration, had been a Sullan protégé. The prosecution gave Cicero the chance to jump on the bandwagon of Pompey, Crassus and those other former lieutenants of Sulla who were busy dismantling their master's reforms. Verres had to be damned, and Cicero did it in style. He was accused of every kind of greed and injustice, of crucifying Roman citizens, of harming the Greek cities of the island which were ancient allies of Rome, of bringing Rome's good name into disrepute. Among the charges and invective, Cicero added tyranny.

> You behaved in the towns and cities of our allies not like a governor sent by the Roman people but like a lustful and cruel tyrant.

Cicero has a good reason for evoking tyranny in these speeches, for Sicily was the proverbial island of tyrants. For reasons that are obscure, the Greek cities of the island had for centuries experienced monarchies of all types. The most famous tyrants of the sixth and fifth centuries were Phalaris and Theron of Akragas, Cleander and Hippocrates of Gela and Gelon of Syracuse. From the fourth century the tyrants of Syracuse dominated the island with only a few periods of intermission until the Roman conquest. The Sicilian tyrants were famous. They built treasuries at Delphi, won chariot races at Olympia and attracted poets and philosophers to their courts. Fabled for their wealth and power, the tyrants of Sicily were also famed for their ruthlessness and cruelty. None was more ferocious than Phalaris of Akragas, who was said to have locked his opponents in a bronze bull and baked them alive. When Cicero in *On Duties* discussed the ethics of tyrannicide he began with the question 'What of Phalaris?'

In the *Verrines*, Cicero tells the story of how after Carthage finally fell to Rome in 146 its conqueror Scipio returned to the Sicilians all the treasures that had been plundered by Carthaginians, including the bronze bull of Phalaris, and asked them whether they preferred to be subject to their own rulers or to the Roman people, now that they possessed this monument to both domestic cruelty and Roman generosity.

⌛

What about tyrannicide itself? For Cicero the words 'tyrant' and 'tyrannicide' were both Greek words, the one unequivocally bad, the other good. For us 'tyrant' remains utterly negative, just as since Caesar's death the Latin word 'dictator' is also pejorative. Both terms were originally neutral, perhaps even positive. Being elected dictator in Rome was an enormous distinction, a sign of the faith placed in one man at a time of national crisis. Tyrants too originally appeared in archaic Greek cities out of periods of conflict, reconciling class struggles, aristocratic faction fighting, regional and ethnic rivalries. But by the fifth century BC tyranny was loathed and hated throughout the classical world. The foun-

10. *The tyrant-slayers that emperors loved to own. This plaster cast depicts a Roman marble copy of a bronze statue-group of the Athenian Tyrannicides, which was itself a replacement for an original pair plundered by Xerxes, the Persian King of Kings. An icon of liberty, the group also evoked the pure and heroic love of the older (bearded) Aristogiton for the youth Harmodius. The marble statues probably adorned gardens belonging to the Roman emperors.*

dation myths of democracy and the *polis* were often steeped in tyrannicide.

Nowhere is this clearer than in the case of Athens, where the tyranny of Peisistratus and his sons dominated politics throughout much of the sixth century. After their fall, everyone disassociated themselves from their rule, even though (or perhaps because) some members of some of the greatest Athenian families had held high office under the tyrants. Athenians revered as founding figures of the classical democracy a pair of young noblemen, Harmodius and Aristogiton, who were often referred to simply as the Tyrannicides. Bronze statues of the pair were set up in the agora, the open public space below the Acropolis that was the centre of civic life. That statue group was plundered from Athens by the Persian emperor Xerxes, and apparently found and returned to Athens by Alexander the Great when he sacked Persepolis nearly two hundred years later. But a replacement group was commissioned and set up within three or four years of the Persian Sack. To judge from this, and from the public cult paid at their tomb and the honours given to their descendants, it might easily be thought that they had brought down the tyranny. And some Athenians apparently did believe this, although others knew that their plan to kill the tyrant Hippias in 514 at the Panathenaic festival was botched and instead his brother Hipparchus was murdered. Aristogiton and Harmodius were executed, and the tyranny lingered for another four years, increasingly paranoid and oppressive, until it was overthrown by a local uprising with outside assistance. In the messy politicking that followed *that* coup, democracy was created as an accidental by-product of the antidote to tyranny. But the Tyrannicides were the most convenient symbols of Athenian liberation. The first Greek historians disputed their roles and motivations, but their cult survived because the democracy needed domestic heroes, and did not want to acknowledge the role played by outside powers or aristocratic families. Hundreds of years later, the Tyrannicides became useful symbols for the Roman republic as it mythologised its own origins in the overthrow of a different tyranny, that of the Tarquins. Pliny the Elder, in his great encyclopedia, puts it succinctly:

These things happened in the same year in which from Rome too the kings were expelled.

The claim that the expulsion of the sons of Peisistratus from Athens coincided exactly with the expulsion of the last kings of Rome shows how Romans had begun to write their own history along Greek lines. And once Roman kings were imagined as tyrants, it was an easy step to seeing Caesar's perpetual dictatorship, and the rumours that he too sought a crown, in terms of that one crime that Cicero said exiled a man from fellowship with all others.

⌛

Aristotle's distinction between good kings and wicked tyrants can be traced back to the hatred that tyranny evoked, in the fifth century BC. Tyrants, it was said, were cruel. They were often lustful. They ruled by fear and with body-guards. Tyrants did not respect the persons of the sons or daughters or wives of the aristocracy. Tyrants slaughtered or exiled the best citizens. Tyranny was opposed to democracy in Aeschylus's *Oresteia*. Sophocles's *Oedipus the Tyrant* played on the hidden hereditary claim to power of the usurper welcomed to Thebes after solving the riddle of the Sphinx. Aristotle represented tyranny as the deviant form of kingship, just as democracy was the deviant form of constitutional government and oligarchy the deviant form of aristocracy. Deviance in each case meant the rulers acting in their own interests, rather than those of the common-wealth. Aristotle further argued that tyrants were most often brought down by their crimes. Rapes and physical assaults often made tyrannicides. Disaffected friends killed some, and others were deposed by the armies of neighbouring states. But above all two reasons drive men against tyrants: hatred and contempt. Although tyrants differed from kings in making themselves powerful by deceit or coercion, kings too might succumb to indulgent and selfish rule, in which case they perished the same way as tyrants did.

Aristotle's political theory is important because it offered a distinction between tyrant and king based not on how the autocrat had come to power, but on how he used it. 'Tyranny,' he writes, 'is monarchy acting in the interests of the monarchy.' Yet he also writes that 'A tyrant arises from the people against the distinguished men so that that people may suffer no ill treatment at their hands.' The implicit distinction between tyranny defined by the mode in which power was gained, and tyranny defined by the way it was wielded, would echo beyond antiquity to Aquinas. Was tyrannicide justified against a ruler who ruled well after usurpation? If a legitimate king overstepped the mark, was regicide acceptable? Shakespeare's *Julius Caesar* shows an awareness of these distinctions. Did Caesar deserve to die because he was already behaving tyrannically? Or was it the fact that he planned to usurp the title of king a better reason to kill him?

⌛

Of the first generation of treatises *On Kingship* that developed Aristotle's thought in the world of the kings, only a little survives. There is a fragment from a preface to a work on rhetoric supposedly addressed to Alexander, and another piece originating in the Jewish community of Ptolemaic Alexandria. Enough survives to show we have the origin of the later genre of mirrors for princes. At first sight they seem laden with flattery, praising the virtues and restraint of kings, but the flattery is persuasive too, offering ideal views of a monarch whose own interests cohere precisely with those of his subjects, who is like a mind to the state's body, reason to the people's passion. The monarch is offered a role close to that of a god, above any laws or constitution. All he has to do is rule well. What sanctions were there if he did not? Absolute monarchs did not depend on the consent of their subjects. But these treatises did, gently and carefully, make clear what happened to kings who did not exercise the proper virtues. They would be regarded and remembered as tyrants, and perhaps even treated as such.

These works advocated restraint, mercy and the art of making peace, and stressed the importance of the education of princes. So far so Platonic. But all the great philosophical schools of the Hellenistic and Roman ages produced treatises on kingship. Epicurus wrote one, also lost, as is that written by Strato the Peripatetic. The only complete ones to have survived were written in the first and second centuries AD – under Rome, that is – and all were products of Stoic thought. At Rome, the senator Musonius Rufus taught on kingship and a summary of his teaching survives under the title *That Kings Too Should Study Philosophy*. The burden of it was that the king must learn to master himself in order to master others. Seneca, the tutor of Nero, wrote a treatise *On Mercy* that acted as a manifesto for the young emperor. Only a little later the Stoic Dio Chrysostom wrote four treatises *On Kingship* for the Emperor Trajan in Greek. Pliny the Younger, his contemporary and another Roman senator, wrote a *Panegyric* of Trajan that also presented him as the ideal king. All of these works focus on the virtues of the king, but all too allow the vices of the tyrant some space, if only for contrast.

Seneca's treatise gives a flavour of their content.

> For mercy makes rulers not only more honoured but also
> safer: it glorifies imperial power at the same time as being
> its surest protection. For what is the reason that kings
> grow old and pass on their power to their children and
> grandchildren, while the power of tyrants is hateful ... and
> shortlived? What difference is there between a king and a
> tyrant? After all they seem alike in eminence and power. Is
> it not that tyrants are savage for their own pleasure's sake,
> while kings only rationally and when absolutely neces-
> sary. 'What is this?' you object. 'Do not kings also execute
> their enemies?' Yes, but only when public interest per-
> suades them to do so. The tyrant has a savage heart. The
> tyrant differs from a king in his deeds, not in name alone.

Arguments of this kind insisted that no king could defend
himself of the charge of tyranny by pointing to his legitimate succession. Seneca emphasises the point. Dionysius
I of Syracuse (who had usurped power) was a better ruler
than many kings. Sulla, although legitimately dictator and
although he resigned that office, still behaved tyrannically.
A list of Sulla's atrocities against Roman citizens demon-
strates his utter lack of mercy. Prominent are the slaughter
of unarmed Roman citizens. Seneca tells the story of how
seven thousand were butchered at one time on his orders
and how Sulla reassured the senate meeting at the time, with
the words, 'Let us carry on with our business, Fathers. It is
just a few dissidents who are dying at my command.'

These ways of thinking about monarchy were already
well known at Rome during the late republic. Romans abroad
were well aware of how kings behaved, and some kings

even visited Rome. But Romans of Brutus's generation also learned about kings and tyrants from the mass of philosophical literature available in Rome, and in conversations with the many Greek intellectuals drawn there by Roman patronage and occasionally coercion. Polybius of Megalopolis, who spent many years as an honoured hostage in Rome in the first half of the second century, included discussion of kingship in his *Universal History*. He subscribed to a development of Aristotle's discussion in the *Politics* that held that there was a cycle of constitutions in which each kind featured, monarchy decaying into tyranny, the overthrow of tyranny giving way to aristocracy which in turn decayed into oligarchy to be replaced first by democracy, then mob rule, before monarchy reasserted itself. For Polybius, the decay of kingship into tyranny gave him a means of understanding how the great Macedonian monarchy of Alexander the Great had given rise to the petty tyrants that Rome had defeated so easily. For Polybius, too, tyranny was a matter of how one ruled, not of how one acquired power in the first place.

By the middle of the first century BC, many Roman aristocrats had studied Greek philosophy and rhetoric in Athens, and some became adherents of one philosophical school or another. Brutus and Cato were Stoics, Caesar and Cassius Epicureans, Cicero was an Academic of a fairly eclectic kind. One of their contemporaries was Lucius Calpurnius Piso Caesoninus, Caesar's father-in-law and sometime political ally, who was consul in 59 BC. It was probably on this occasion that the Epicurean philosopher Philodemus of Gadara dedicated to Piso a treatise *On the Good King According to Homer*, a treatise partly preserved when Piso's villa outside Herculaneum was covered in mud by the same eruption of Vesuvius that buried Pompeii. Philodemus makes use of incidents from the *Odyssey* and the *Iliad* to advocate a particular style of ruling. The Good King is as wise as Odysseus or Nestor, not as arrogant as Agamemnon nor as proud as Achilles. He respects others' property and the natural world, he does not commit murders and he is clement. Like all Epicureans, Philodemus advocated controlling the passions. Like Cicero in *On Duties* he advised Piso on how to win support through friendship. The Good King resolves disputes, soothes passions, and of course he is not a tyrant. Piso's villa was decorated with portraits of Hellenistic kings. The greatest monarchs of the third century BC had entertained philosophers at their courts. By the first century Rome had supplanted them as the centre of Greek cultural life. Just as Epicurus had once advised the kings of Macedon and Thrace, now Philodemus lived with Piso and travelled with him, and was well known to the Latin intelligentsia of the capital, Cicero and Virgil among them.

Many of these ideas lay dormant in Rome, like seeds awaiting the moment to germinate. That moment was the dictatorship of Caesar. Caesar's own advertisement of his mercy may have been inspired by similar treatises to that of Philodemus. Perhaps Brutus and the other conspirators used philosophical discussions of tyranny to measure Caesar's behaviour. But they did not wish to choose between kingship and tyranny, but between freedom and the rule of one man. Cicero's complaints in *On Duties* condemn Caesar not only for the way he exercised supreme power, but for the fact that he did. All the same, Cicero found a use for Kingship theory on the first occasion when he publicly spoke before Caesar the dictator, in a speech seeking the return from exile of Caesar's enemy Marcus Claudius Marcellus.

After Cato's suicide in April 46, Marcellus was the most

prominent of Caesar's enemies not yet reconciled to him. Many of the other former Pompeians, Brutus and Cassius among them, already had provinces or commands. Cicero had been forgiven. Marcellus had been a bitter opponent of Caesar since his consulship in 51. Then he had criticised Caesar's grants of citizenship in northern Italy, and he later proposed recalling Caesar from Gaul and giving his armies to someone else. He was one of Pompey's senior supporters, and after Pharsalus he fled to the Greek city of Mitylene. Now, with the dictator demonstrating his mercy and speaking of reconciliation, the time seemed right to bring Marcellus home. The matter was raised in the senate by Philodemus's patron, Caesar's father-in-law, Piso. The deal was brokered behind closed doors. In September 46 Cicero agreed to break his self-imposed silence to formally thank Caesar. He began with a catalogue of royal virtues:

> Such humanity, such unaccustomed and unheard of mercy, such moderation from one with supreme power over all things, indeed such unbelievable and almost divine wisdom.

Cicero moved rapidly from addressing the gathered senators to addressing Caesar himself, praising his formal restitution of Marcellus (made after cataloguing the wrongs Caesar had suffered at his hands) before going on to eulogise Caesar's achievements. Alongside his conquests of barbarian nations Cicero sets Caesar's conquest of his own passions, and proclaims him godlike. His justice and mercy outshone his military trophies and monuments. Caesar has proved his claim that he entered civil war unwillingly. Like Philodemus's Good King, in other words, Caesar was a peacemaker, a resolver of disputes and reluctant and restrained in his use of force. Cicero, no doubt sincerely, praised the lack of civilian casualties of the kind that had characterised Sulla's dictatorship. But he then moved on to advise Caesar on his future conduct. Don't become weary of preserving the state, rejoice in the glory virtuous action brings, restore the law-courts and the citizen body. Do not rest until you have established the commonwealth in good order. And bear in mind the judgement of posterity.

⧗

Between the senate meeting at which Cicero hailed Caesar as almost a god, and that other meeting at which Caesar was slaughtered, stretched a year and a half. Marcellus himself never made it back to Rome. He set out from Mytilene and crossed the Aegean, but when he reached the port of Athens in May of 45 BC he was attacked and murdered by one of his attendants. No motive is recorded. Meanwhile Caesar followed the regal and godlike path that Cicero had mapped out for him. Perhaps no one knew where it would lead. Some of Cicero's language maybe hints at the hope that, his work done, Caesar would resign the dictatorship as Sulla had done. Cicero mentioned, and deplored, rumours of conspiracy against him. A veiled threat? Or a warning that praise was conditional, like the closing injunction to Caesar to think of the ultimate verdict history would pass on him? More positively Cicero had spoken of reconstructing the commonwealth as the one remaining task facing Caesar before he could enjoy the fruits of his labour in peace and leisure. But Caesar was surely right that Sulla's resignation had been a mistake. Sulla the Dictator's work of reconstruction was reversed in a decade, leaving only his reputation for savagery. Why should Caesar's popular reforms be treated more kindly?

Yet kingship did not seem to be an option either, at least not in Rome. By Caesar's day it was widely believed that the Roman state, like the Athenian democracy, was founded in the expulsion of tyrants. Stories of the last kings of Rome, the Tarquins, clothed them in the familiar tyrannical costume of arrogance and cruelty. Tyranny did not end with the expulsion of Tarquin the Proud. There is the tale of the death of another innocent aristocratic maiden, Verginia, slain by her father to stop her falling into the hands of a home-grown tyrant, Appius Claudius. Then there is the story of Horatius holding the bridge against an Etruscan army led by Lars Porsena of Clusium to reimpose Etruscan overlordship of Rome. More shadowy accounts surround Spurius Cassius, said to have proposed land distributions and been executed for aiming at kingship in 486 BC. Spurius Maelius distributed grain in a crisis and allegedly tried to make himself tyrant in 439 BC but was assassinated by Gaius Servilius Ahala. Marius Manlius was executed for tyrannical ambitions after he proposed debt relief in 385. Cicero had no compunction about adding the name of Tiberius Gracchus to this list.

Stories of tyrannicide in archaic Rome certainly circulated as early as the second century BC. Many Romans believed them, and some were perhaps even true. After all, the early Roman state must have been quite like the Greek cities in which tyrants had arisen, and there is some evidence for figures rather like tyrants in some Etruscan cities. Rome was not far from the nearest Greek tyrannies. Aristodemus, tyrant of Greek Cumae just north of Naples, fought with the same Lars Porsena in 504 BC. Tarquin the Proud sheltered at his court after his expulsion from Rome. On the other hand, perhaps the Roman narratives were shaped by Greek traditions. Either way, tyrannicide was established in the Roman tradition too as a virtuous act. If archaic Rome had vicious tyrants it also had virtuous kings: Romulus the original founder was the son of Mars and revered as a god, while Numa the second king and Servius Tullius the sixth provided other founder figures, for public religion, and for the Roman army respectively.

Cicero's *Republic*, written in the mid-fifties BC, represents his hero, the general Scipio, expressing a philosophically conventional preference for monarchy, so long as the ruler was a man of moral excellence. But in the end he concluded that a constitution that mixed the best elements of autocracy, aristocracy and democracy was the most stable.

> For beneath the tolerable or if you prefer even likeable King Cyrus, to name just the most prominent example, savage Phalaris is ready to drive him to a change of character. Absolute power vested in a single man easily and quickly degenerates into a tyranny like his.

Cicero's Scipio subscribes to a version of the same cycle of constitutions as Polybius. The transition from Romulus to Tarquin the Proud marks the decay from a good king, a civiliser of barbarians and founder of the city's institutions, to the hateful arrogance of the tyrant. Yet Scipio and his interlocutors in the dialogue repeatedly state that the name of king is now hateful to the Roman people. Scipio's regal history seems at times a struggle between an elective monarchy in which kings were chosen for their virtue, and the claims of a hereditary kingship. Tarquinius Priscus is the son of a Corinthian exile, a man who had fled the tyranny of the Cypselids and settled in the Etruscan city of Tarquinii. Moving to Rome, he

11. Brutus, as Michelangelo imagined him in 1540, perhaps in an allusion to the the assassination of Duke Alessandro de Medici who had, in Michelangelo's view, enslaved his native Florence much as Caesar had Rome.

became a friend of King Ancus Martius, a grandson of Numa, and when Ancus died he was elected by the people to succeed him. Like every other king 'he initiated sound and useful institutions'. But he was killed by the sons of Ancus Martius. Servius Tullius succeeded him and ruled well, defeating Rome's enemies and setting up the popular assemblies. But he was murdered and supplanted by another Tarquin, the last king and tyrant par excellence. Tarquin's lack of self-control and his resort to terror mark him out as a classic tyrant as much as do his crimes and those of his son. Scipio continues, pointing out the transformation of constitutions that results:

The result was that a man of outstanding intellect and virtue, Lucius Brutus, freed his fellow citizens from the unjust yoke of their harsh slavery. Although he was a private citizen he sustained the whole of the commonwealth, and he was the first of us to show that no man is without public responsibility when it is a matter of safeguarding the freedom of the citizen body.

The lesson that Scipio draws about the difference between a king and a tyrant – and he uses the Greek term and refers to Greek discussions at this point – is that no creature is more monstrous or disgraceful than a tyrant, no creature more hateful to gods and men, and that a tyrant had put himself outside the human community.

Here then, already a decade before Caesar's assassination, we find that fusion of Roman legendary traditions and Greek Kingship theory that provided the conspirators with a charter for the assassination of a tyrant. From this mixture of myth, philosophy and politics had been fashioned the means of telling a good autocrat from a bad one, along with the justification for killing any tyrant. Cicero in *On Duties* has not changed his tune. The experience of Caesar's dictatorship may have hardened his line, and it gave him examples from recent history rather than Roman myth. But the verdict remained the same. Tyranny was the exceptional crime. For the sake of civility and law, to protect property and the innocent, in the name of freedom and the Roman aristocracy, the tyrant had to die. Does this seem a messy argumentation, based on bad history, ancestral prejudice and ill-concealed interest? But who are we to judge, when our own leaders make equally bad cases for the exceptional murder that will preserve our rational and civil societies free from violence?

3

CAESAR'S MURDERED HEIRS

The Ides of March are a bottleneck in Roman history. Picture the Roman past like an hourglass. From above presses down the mass of history, from now obscure origins in myth and legend down through the rise of Rome in Italy, and the sand rushes faster as Rome defeats great Carthage and the Kings and then makes the world her own. At home increasingly violent political disturbances grow into full-scale civil wars alternating with the suppressed violence of juntas. Caesar's death is the end of that story. Below the neck of the hourglass, the domination of Augustus broadens out into the imperial peace, emperor following emperor, tyrants and kings alike, for five hundred years until the fall of Rome, fifteen hundred until the fall of Byzantium, nearly two thousand before the fall of last emperors whose titles and symbols preserved echoes of the slaughtered dictator's name into the twentieth century. The imperial eagles of Napoleon, Russia and the Austro-Hungarian empire look back to Rome; so too does the elaborate imperial titulature of Victoria of India, Maximilian of Mexico and Bokassa of the Congo. The first of all these Caesars, Czars and Kaisers was Julius the Dictator.

Republic did not turn into empire in a day, naturally. Perhaps the free republic Cicero idolised had been dead before he ever entered politics. Cicero sometimes blamed the

Gracchi, others felt the world changed when Sulla first led Roman soldiers into Rome. Maybe the rule of the emperors was not secure until on Augustus's death in AD 14 his power was passed on to his adopted son Tiberius. Other landmarks were the failure of the senate to restore the republic when the emperor Caligula was assassinated in 41 AD and the survival of the institution of monarchy beyond the suicide of the last Julio-Claudian, Nero, in 68. But around the centre of this long century of torments lies Caesar's murder. The Tiberian scholar Cremutius Cordus called Brutus and Cassius the last of the Romans. For Suetonius, Julius was the first of the Caesars. Both were correct.

Yet Caesar's assassination was a failure. If it was intended to free the state from monarchy and restore freedom to the senatorial aristocracy, it did neither. Before Cicero's death, he had seen new tyrants arise whom he condemned far more ferociously than he had Caesar. Romans fought Romans again in the campaigns leading up to Philippi in 42 BC, again in a short conflict at Perugia between Octavian's supporters and Antony's, in the campaigns against Pompey's son Sextus and yet again in the often postponed showdown between Antony and Octavian at the battle of Actium in 31.

Yet Caesar's death did make a difference. After the battle of Actium it was almost a hundred years before the next Roman civil war, one that lasted less than two years. Domitian, the third emperor of the new Flavian dynasty, was assassinated thirty-odd years later, but a peaceful succession was somehow managed. In fact civil war did not break out again until the murder of Commodus in AD 192. It took a little longer this time to restore order: the last battle was fought in 197. But the Severan dynasty lasted until 235 before the empire again dissolved into half a century of fragmentation, usurpation and chaos. But for more than two and a half centuries Rome held civil war at bay. Gibbon's famous Golden Age lies at the heart of this period. When conflicts did take place they were mostly fought between the legions, usually far from Rome. Civil war lurked in the Roman imagination like a recurrent nightmare that surfaced in epic poetry or in the cult of Brutus, Cassius and Cato. There was, of course, opposition and sporadic tyranny. Senators were executed and others instructed to take their own lives. None had the freedom of speech enjoyed even by Cicero, whose published speeches were now school-texts and classics. But there were no proscriptions, no mass murders, almost no conflict in the city itself. The lives of the elite were predictable and for the most part secure.

Except, that is, for the assassination of emperors, constantly plotted, the subject of intense rumour and successful over and over again. As one historian recently put it, 'Emperors don't die in bed.' How had assassination, which once plunged the Roman world into chaos, become part of the new order of things? Was there a connection between the frequency of tyrannicide and the rarity of civil violence? Frazer famously began *The Golden Bough*, the founding tract of anthropology, with the story of the priest of Nemi, the great sanctuary in the Alban Hills just outside Rome. Each priest was an escaped slave who had murdered his predecessor, and would be priest until he in turn was murdered by his successor. Had the Caesars unwittingly taken on the burden of the Dying King, their successive assassinations securing what Pliny called the immeasurable majesty of the Roman peace? Roman writers too wondered about these things, and added new chapters to Cicero's anatomy of regicide.

⧗

Augustus himself did manage to die in his bed. The second emperor Tiberius hid away on Capri for most of the latter part of his reign. Rumour had it that he was murdered there by the prefect of the praetorian guard – the crack corps whose function was to protect the emperor – to ensure the succession of Caligula, who lasted only four years before he was assassinated, again by guardsmen. His uncle Claudius was allegedly poisoned by a dish of mushrooms provided by his wife and niece Agrippina. Nero's reign ended in chaos, provincial rebellions triggering a mass defection of senators and a fatal loss of nerve. Fleeing the City, Nero sheltered in the house of one of his ex-slaves and killed himself there. During the civil war of 68–9 three emperors, Galba, Otho and Vitellius, all perished violently. Galba was killed by praetorians in favour of Otho. The eventual victor Vespasian did manage a natural death. His eldest son Titus probably did the same, although there were rumours of poisoning. His brother Domitian fell victim to a palace conspiracy. His successor Nerva, old when appointed, narrowly avoided a coup by adopting the most likely usurper Trajan. His death too seems to have been natural. Hadrian, Antoninus and Marcus all evaded any conspiracies planned for them. It was not until Commodus that another emperor perished at an assassin's hands. Commodus's successor Pertinax was murdered by the praetorians who then auctioned off the empire to the highest bidder. When Severus came to power he disbanded them and filled their ranks with his loyal legionaries. Order was only temporarily restored. Few of Severus's successors died naturally.

For every successful murder, there were a mass of failed

attempts. Seneca, in his essay *On the Shortness of Life*, lists the plots faced by Augustus as he set the state in order and pushed out the boundaries of the empire beyond the Rhine, the Euphrates and the Danube.

> Meanwhile in Rome itself the daggers of Murena, of Caepio, of Lepidus, of Egnatius and others were being sharpened against him. No sooner had he escaped their plots than his own daughter and so many young aristocrats, bound to her by adultery as if by an oath, threatened his old age. Then there was the plot of Paulus to be feared, and another Antony in alliance with another woman.

The conspiracy led by Marcus Aemilius Lepidus took place in 30 BC, that of Murena and Caepio in 23 or 22 BC, and that of Egnatius Rufus in 19 BC. The alleged plots surrounding Augustus's own daughter Julia were exposed in 2 BC: those of her daughter, in which Aemilius Paulus and Iullus Antonius were implicated, took place eight years later.

The plots against Augustus's life in the early part of his reign are also mentioned by Tacitus, Suetonius and Pliny the Elder. Most similar to the conspiracy that killed Caesar was that plot of Marcus Lepidus, son of Caesar's Master of Horse and of Brutus's sister. Velleius says the plan was to kill Octavian on his return to Rome after Antony's defeat, and that it was discovered by Augustus's trusted lieutenant Maecenas, left in charge of the city during his absence, and dealt with at once to avoid rekindling the civil war. Once again we see conspiracy germinating within the heart of the Roman aristocracy, where personal, political and principled reasons for assassination tangled confusingly. But there is a shift in the nature of conspiracy over the first emperor's long reign. Towards the end of Augustus's life, the focus of tension became the matter of the succession. Rumour surrounded struggles within the imperial house. Augustus's grandson Agrippa Postumus was exiled for viciousness, but there was a story that Augustus had not long before his death visited the island of his exile in search of reconciliation. Postumus's murder on the order of Tiberius immediately after Augustus's death was, according to Tacitus, the 'first crime of the new principate'. Rome has made the transition to a new style of murder, one that originates from within the court, not from its enemies.

Part of the transformation of republic into empire was that the inner circle from which most plots emerged was more and more focused on the palace and less and less on the senate. But the distinction is not absolute, in fact the Roman monarchy is unusual and unlike its Hellenistic counterparts in that the aristocracy were so much part of the court society. Emperors and their relatives always married aristocrats, and the greatest of their friends were senators or members of the equestrian order, Rome's junior aristocracy. Naturally, it was to them they turned for advice and assistance. And when emperors lacked heirs of their own kin their successors were always drawn from the senate.

This evolution from aristocratic republic to aristocratic court was not a smooth one. Honour itself, and that fearsome Roman *dignitas* for which Caesar had gone to war, were at stake. During the twenties two great aristocrats fell from grace over this sort of dispute, one the grandson of Caesar's sometime ally Crassus, the other one of Caesar's closest friends. Both were governors and commanders of legions. The former had demanded the *spolia opima*, an honour given only to a general who had killed an enemy leader in single combat: this was so rare that it had been awarded only three times in Roman history. The latter had advertised his own virtues too ostentatiously in his province of Egypt. All this would have been conventional a few decades before: now the emperor's family would monopolise the greatest ceremonials, and aristocrats would receive only the honours that he bestowed. Resentment at this may have been one motivation behind the attempted coups of Murena and Caepio and that of Egnatius Rufus, whose career as a popular candidate was curtailed by Augustus. Velleius even called him a second Catiline. Yet the Roman court was institutionalised soon enough. The conventions were more or less laid down by the end of Augustus's reign, the reigns of his immediate successors saw some experimentation by emperors and their aristocrat courtiers alike, and by Trajan's day a mass of rituals, protocols and manners had emerged. When Pliny the Younger, following custom, addressed a speech of thanks and praise to the emperor for his consulship, he far surpassed Cicero's speech *For Marcellus*. 'Command us to be free, Master, and we shall be!'

What of freedom then? Brutus had called out 'freedom' as Caesar lay dying and Tacitus provocatively claimed freedom was born with the republic when the kings were expelled. This is not the *liberté* of the French Revolution, a freedom for all citizens coterminous with equality and brotherhood. *Libertas* for Roman aristocrats meant freedom to fulfil their political ambitions, under the law but without being subjected to anyone else's power, and even Augustus could claim to have restored the *libertas* of the Roman state after it had been oppressed by the domination of a faction. Freedom, that is, to compete for honours. Tacitus on another occasion called Nerva the first emperor to combine liberty and the principate. Monarchy was compatible with freedom, so long as the ruler was not a tyrant. The trouble was, so many emperors turned out to be tyrants ...

⧗

What was imperial tyranny like, then, and how was it opposed in imperial Rome? Consider the case of Domitian, emperor from 13 September AD 81 until his assassination on 18 September AD 96. Fifteen years was a fairly long reign for a Roman emperor and Domitian's was marked by military and financial successes. But all of that was undone by the events of his last day, together with the fact that there was no heir from the Flavian house to succeed him.

A great life-size bronze statue was recently dragged up from the sea at Miseno, just north of Naples. It portrays a bare-headed emperor wearing a breastplate, urging his horse on into battle. This sort of image of a warrior king harked back to Alexander the Great. One equestrian statue of Alexander, with his head replaced by that of Julius Caesar, stood in Caesar's forum before the temple of Venus the Ancestress. The motif recurs again and again in Roman art. Marcus Aurelius rides a great bronze charger in the Capitoline Museum in Rome. The type of an emperor trampling diminutive barbarians underfoot is one of the commonest designs on coins of the early empire. The court poet Statius composed a poem eulogising a bronze equestrian statue of Domitian set up in the Roman forum. The poem stands at the head of the first book of Statius's *Silvae*. It begins:

What mass is this that grips the Latin Forum, twinned by

12. *The emperor Domitian. Unlike many images of this emperor, this bust, now in the Capitoline Museum in Rome, escaped mutilation after Domitian's murder.*

the colossus mounted on its back? Did this masterpiece descend ready made from heaven? Or was it forged in the volcanoes of Sicily, exhausting its Cyclopian smiths? Or was it Athena that made this for you, Germanicus, a perfect image of you clutching the reins, just as the Rhine and the mountains of Transylvania saw you in the flesh?

Domitian was a warrior emperor. His father Vespasian and elder brother Titus had won the Jewish war, bringing back booty and prisoners to build the Colosseum on the site where Nero had built his fabulous Golden House. Domitian's campaigns were in northern Europe, first advancing the Roman frontier in Germany – hence the title Germanicus – and then campaigning against the Dacians who inhabited the western part of modern Romania. Domitian was equally a great patron of the arts. Statius was just one of a generation of brilliant poets, many of whom came to Rome to compete in the great Capitoline games that he founded, the first regular contest in Rome to be organised in the Greek fashion with music, poetry and athletics rather than gladiators, beast hunts or chariot racing. The games were dedicated to the goddess Minerva, the Roman Athena, whom Domitian adopted as a patron.

If Domitian had lived longer, or been succeeded by a blood relative, it is easy to imagine him receiving some of the same praises showered on Trajan who adopted the title *Optimus Princeps*, Best of Princes. But it was Trajan who would be remembered for renewing Rome's conquest of the world, Trajan whose Dacian booty would beautify the city and restore Italian prosperity, and Trajan who would be idolised as affable, approachable, charming and just. All this too could have been Domitian's posterity. But the statue at Miseno lacks a face, or rather its face has been crudely removed and replaced with another, that of Nerva. The join is as obvious as the stitchmarks on the face of Frankenstein's monster. This is neither an accident, nor a sign of clumsy craftsmanship. More important than the display of loyalty to Nerva was a visible symbol of the rejection of Domitian. Historians, orators and satirists followed suit. The Domitian of ancient accounts is most often a tyrant, he is firmly inscribed among the Bad Emperors. Pliny cast him in his *Panegyric* as the tyrant whose vices made Trajan even more clearly a king.

13. *Another Domitian ... at least until the face of this spectacular bronze recently found at Miseno was cut away and replaced with that of his successor Nerva.*

Reconstructing the historical Domitian is not easy, but it is essential in showing how assassination could destroy an emperor's reputation as well as his life. Most ancient biographers believed that a person's nature was more or less fixed, visible in the most trivial anecdote and evident from an early age. Domitian's vices feature at the beginning of both the main accounts of him that have survived, a biography written by the Hadrianic courtier Suetonius and one book, now sadly abbreviated by Byzantine scholars, of an epic history of Rome's first thousand years written under the Severi by the distinguished Bithynian Greek senator Cassius Dio. Suetonius's Domitian is indeed a monster from childhood. His principal vice was cruelty, although lust too features in some anecdotes. He had crucified not only an historian who had made some uncomplimentary references to him, but also the poor slaves who had copied out the work. He took part in the torture of his enemies, inventing new ways of inflicting pain. He used to depilate his mistresses personally, and after refusing his niece when she was a virgin seduced her once she was married to someone else. Domitian's successes are disposed of early in the life (out of chronological order, that is) and Suetonius presents the emergence of the latent tyrant only later, with his true viciousness emerging most clearly only after a failed coup in 89 AD.

Cassius Dio offers what must once have been a much better account, but even so Domitian displays some of the stereotypical qualities of a tyrant. He was untrustworthy and secretive, given to bouts of savage anger and also sinister smouldering resentment. He celebrated splendid games for Minerva at his Alban Villa. It was always the sign of a bad emperor that he did in private what good ones did in public, and Pliny too criticises Domitian for lurking away from the public gaze to which Trajan submitted himself easily. Domitian cared for almost no one, although he pretended friendship to those he was about to attack. Tacitus had attacked the emperor Tiberius for always concealing his animosities. Domitian even turned against his informers, and hated those who had been friends of his father and brother. Senators always feared the redistributions of favour that accompanied changes of emperor: abandoning the old retainers of the Flavian family was a heinous crime. Even Domitian's more praiseworthy acts are given a sinister spin. Confirming the acts and gifts of his father and brother is represented by Dio as a mere show, and Domitian's prohibition of castration is made an obscure slight on his dead brother who was allegedly fond of eunuchs. But Dio has the courtier's eye for the hypocrisies of the vulgar tradition. He criticised the senate for insisting that Domitian not execute any senator who had not been condemned by his peers. Tacitus, on the other hand, had lamented his forced participation in show trials in the senate that preceded the execution of dissidents. Had Dio's own experience of the way Severus dealt with his enemies made him regard the senate of a hundred years before as naïve? The debate obscures the fact that there were not, in fact, many executions of senators under Domitian. Dio and Suetonius both admit many were simply exiled or even pardoned. Given their hostility to Domitian, we can be sure that any real bloodbath would have received full coverage. The truth is that Domitian was relatively moderate. And all emperors executed traitors, even Trajan …

Domitian's tyranny was illustrated by specific charges, that he nearly executed his wife for adultery, that he did have an actor killed because of her, that he cohabited with his niece even after reconciling with his wife. Like all ancient writers, Dio plays down the success of Domitianic campaigns in Germany. This is Trajanic propaganda which the archaeology of the Roman frontier refutes. Likewise Dio ridicules the honours and titles showered on Domitian, and claims that he both demanded and despised flattery. Domitian paid little respect to senatorial protocol, monopolised the senior magistracies, pandered to the people with extravagant games, funded from the property of rich men executed on trumped-up charges. Domitian's triumphs, honours and games were ridiculed. While the people were fêted, the senators and knights were tormented, treated to a triumphal banquet arranged like a funeral feast with a tombstone marking each space. Some at least of this reflects a common pattern. Emperors who, like Caligula and Claudius and Hadrian, took liberties with the honours and prerogatives that senators felt were their due tended to receive very negative appraisals. Domitian may not have allowed the senate its accustomed share of honour and prestige. But he wielded no greater power than did Trajan. And Trajan, like Domitian, was addressed as *Domine,* a term which almost always expressed subservience.

The shadow of Domitian's eventual assassination hangs over all this narrative. So compelling are the cumulated anecdotes that many modern writers have taken it for granted that Domitian was killed because he was a tyrant. Yet it is equally possible that he came to be recognised as a tyrant partly because he was killed. Perhaps neither the failed military coup of 89 nor the assassination that succeeded commanded widespread support. All emperors attracted animosity and made enemies. Domitian reflected thoughtfully on this. He said that emperors who did not punish many of their subjects were not better than the others, just luckier. And he even understood that his subjects could not be expected to share this view. According to Suetonius:

> He used to say that the position of an emperor was a most miserable one, because nothing he said about discovering assassination attempts was ever believed until after he had been murdered in one.

The first serious opposition to Domitian of which we hear was a botched military uprising led by the governor of Upper (southern) Germany in January 89. Lucius Antonius Saturninus was quickly defeated by the governor of the province of Lower (northern) Germany, Aulus Bucius Lappius Maximus. Dio praised him for burning the rebel's correspondence, which might have revealed who else had been involved. Loyal troops came to Maximus's aid from neighbouring provinces but the revolt was crushed before either Domitian and the praetorian guard could arrive from Rome, or the seventh legion from Spain led by the future emperor Trajan.

Not much is known about the causes of this rebellion, and nothing of Saturninus's motives. Domitian was generally popular with the military, as most campaigning emperors were. After his assassination the troops were outraged, called for his deification and would have avenged him if possible. Suetonius suggests that Domitian himself thought that basing two legions in the same camp and keeping a mass of accumulated cash there had put temptation in their commander's way: the emperor took steps to prevent this happening again. Suetonius also claims that German allies were about to cross the Rhine to help Saturninus and only the melting of the ice that covered the river prevented them! Perhaps rumour was already elaborating on a conflict the details of which Domitian wanted to keep obscure. The chance factor of the involvement of Trajan as a loyal supporter of Domitian ensured that Saturninus was not destined to be hailed as a martyr in future reigns.

But if the origin of the revolt is obscure, many things about it are not surprising. Most obviously there is the location. Since early in Augustus's reign the total number of troops in the legions had been kept low. By Severus's reign it had crept up from twenty-four to thirty legions, but with only 5,000 men in each, and many of them understrength, the total remained under 150,000 men supported by probably about the same number of irregular troops. An army of 300,000 was a tiny number to guard a frontier as long as that of the empire, or indeed to control a subject population of between 50 and 100 million. The only way it could be done was to develop a spectacularly effective system of communications – signal towers, relays of horses, fleets and Rome's famous roads, all humming with messengers carrying intelligence reports, records and orders – a system that enabled troops to be concentrated rapidly wherever they were needed.

During the first few centuries of the empire the key military concentrations were in the Rhineland, where up to a third of the army was at times deployed; in the Danube provinces that stretched from the Alps to the Black Sea; and in Syria. The first two armies faced the northern barbarians, to begin with the next regions scheduled for conquest, eventually those from which raids and invasions were most feared. The Syrian army watched over the frontier with the Persian empire, as well as dealing with sporadic violence in Judaea. Over the next century, the only change to this situation was the creation of an army of three legions in Britain. These were the only conceivable power-bases for a full-scale military coup. The praetorian guards in Rome might offer important support for a coup, but only if conflict did not escalate to the point where the legions became involved. Alexandria and its prefect offered help to Vespasian, but it was the allegiance of the Syrian and Danube armies that ensured his ultimate victory over Vitellius with his German legions. The Severi depended on the Danube legions in their civil war, but they had to defeat rivals backed by the armies of Syria and Britain before they were secure. Failed revolts tell the same story. The first military revolt the emperors faced was in Claudius's reign and was led by the generals of the Danube army. But the legions refused to march against a Caesar. Their reward included the regimental titles Pious and Faithful. Domitian awarded the same titles to the loyal legions of Lower Germany. Trajan was rewarded for his loyalty to Domitian with a consulship and a German command: it was the latter which persuaded Nerva to adopt him when his own reign got into trouble. The Syrian command was the basis for a failed revolt led by the great general Avidius Cassius in 175 AD, who was apparently under the impression that Marcus Aurelius was dead.

Military rebellions almost always did fail. There were two main reasons. First, almost every emperor since Augustus had worked hard to build links with the troops independent of the line of command. Soldiers received gifts on imperial accessions and anniversaries, gifts paid in coin which often celebrated the military achievements of the emperors. Sensible emperors made sure that they and their sons, sometimes even their wives, travelled to the camps and met the legions. Germanicus stifled a mutiny by holding up his children before the troops. Agrippina had the title Mother of the Camps. And the soldiers worshipped the emperors as gods. At Maryport in Cumbria a series of altars testify to annual vows for the emperor of the kind governors made in their provinces. A military calendar from the garrison town of Dura on the Euphrates shows how many holidays were linked to anniversaries of the imperial house, celebrations of the birthdays of imperial princes and of the anniversaries of the dates on which they had put on the toga of manhood and so on. Images of the emperors were lodged in the centre of each legionary camp alongside the eagles: both received cult. This paid off in terms of loyalty. When Scribonianus tried to get his troops to march against Claudius the standards were difficult to remove from their turf altars: the troops took it as an omen and stood down. Domitian learned of the failure of Saturninus's revolt when a great eagle alighted on the emperor's statue at Rome shrieking news of victory. For many soldiers, as for many others in the empire, the emperors were gods. Marching against them was a terrifying prospect.

The second obstacle was the fragmentation of the Roman elite, the only body from which any plausible successor could emerge. Across the empire at any one time there were up to thirty senators commanding legions, and about as many governing provinces. Then from the second aristocracy, the equestrian order, there were a clutch of governors of the smaller provinces, the commanders of the greatest fleets, the prefect of Alexandria and Egypt and a few dozen procurators who managed tax collection and imperial property of various kinds. In Rome there were the rest of the senators, four or five hundred in theory, and the commanders of the praetorian guard and of the urban cohorts. Staging a coup meant forming some sort of consensus among all these. After Caligula's assassination in 41 AD the senate actually did meet and began a debate on the accession. Pointlessly. The praetorians found the dead emperor's fifty-year-old uncle and whisked him away to their camp to proclaim him emperor, a moment immortalised by Derek Jacobi in *I Claudius*. There were to be nervous months ahead for those who had been front runners in the senatorial debate.

If the senate was useless, it would have to be a junta among the generals. This is the way that the Flavian coup had taken place. Those generals left out in the cold when it seemed as if the army of Germany would seize Rome rapidly conferred. Letters and envoys rushed back and forth between the military bases and the seats of the governors. A Vitellian victory might cost them their commands and rewards in the form of future consulships that Vitellian supporters would certainly enjoy. The leaders of the Danubian and Syrian armies apparently resolved on a coup even before they had a candidate. One of Vespasian's strongest cards was a pair of adult sons, Titus and Domitian. Backing the Flavians meant buying a dynasty. So while Vespasian secured Alexandria and the grain of Egypt, and received omens of his future greatness in the temple of Serapis, Danubian troops marched down into Italy preparing the way for a relatively bloodless arrival of the next emperor. Their commanders would hold many of the consulships of the following decade. What letters of sympathy or support were in the postbag of Saturninus that Maximus destroyed we can only guess. This is the stuff of rumour. When Avidius Cassius revolted he tried to persuade the Athenian millionaire Herodes to join him. The story goes that Herodes sent back a one-word letter, *'emaneis'*, Greek for 'You have gone mad.'

Maybe Domitian too could only guess what support Saturninus had had, or who had been waiting undecided in the wings. Dio and Suetonius both claim that this was the beginning of a reign of terror. It is not easy to substantiate this claim, and Domitian did not exclude his fiercest critics from high office. There were in fact few executions. Domitian seems to have tried a more subtle approach to retaining power. He had himself made censor – making him guardian of morals, and giving him the traditional means of revising the register of senators. He seized the moral high ground as Augustus had, by cracking down on adultery, expelling philosophers from the city and punishing atheists and senators who had fought as gladiators. There was temple building, and priestesses of Vesta who had broken their vows to preserve their virginity were punished. Both the Vestals and their lovers were drawn from the most noble families in Rome. None of this makes much sense in terms of the familiar narrative of a panicked descent into despotism following a failed coup. That story arc, of course, belongs to the trope of tyranny at least as far back as the expulsion of the Peisistratids from Athens. It looks more as though we are observing a struggle for moral authority. The censorship had always been a powerful weapon against the rich, and philosophers had been among the most vocal critics of Nero and Vespasian before Domitian. Was Domitian putting the senate under gentle pressure?

The plot that finally resulted in Domitian's assassination originated in any case not with senators but within his court. His own ex-slaves were at its centre, preparing a plot against him in his private chambers. Roman generals of the republic had relied heavily on the senior slaves and former slaves of their own household to manage their public and private affairs alike. Rome had no real civil service, and slaves were bound to their masters even after they had been freed. One of the most valuable parts of Octavian's inheritance from Julius Caesar was his household: when he became the first emperor and took the title Augustus, he used slaves and ex-slaves as confidential ministers. Wise emperors kept their dependence on their domestics quiet – although it was an open secret – because aristocrats loathed kowtowing to slaves. But a slave could never replace an emperor while an aristocrat could, so they were always needed. Emperors like Claudius, whose relations with the senate were exceptionally bad, would parade their slaves and ex-slaves in public, and award them honours normally reserved for the nobles. Senatorial writers responded by accusing Claudius of being in his slaves' power. But no emperor could do without them, and that dependence came with a price-tag.

The ex-slaves Parthenius, Sigerus, Entellus and Stephanus are named as the main plotters by Dio. Domitian's wife, the praetorian prefects and in one account the future emperor Nerva were also implicated. Is all this plausible, given how much these courtiers depended on Domitian for their position? Dio tells a strange story that Domitian had written some sort of memo to himself to have them killed, a memo which was found and stolen by a slave and brought to the empress. But Dio also claims that the conspiracy was already being planned and the memo only accelerated its implementation, and also that Domitian was in any case already killing prominent men named as his enemies in a prophesy. Another possible motive is that Domitian had begun to crack down on abuses committed by his own freedmen. When he discovered that one of them had stolen stone destined for rebuilding the temple of Capitoline Jupiter and used it to build a tomb for his son, Domitian had the tomb demolished and the bones thrown into the sea. Epaphroditus, one of Nero's infamous ex-slaves, was executed allegedly to remind the emperor's own freedmen that they were not invulnerable. Had the inner circle become afraid for its position? Claudius's freedmen were credited with organizing the fall of his second wife Messalina in order to preserve their influence. Suetonius has a completely different story, finding the origins of the conspiracy in a struggle over the succession. Domitian had no surviving brothers and his son had died in infancy. Rumour had it that he impregnated his niece, but that she died during the abortion he forced on her. According to Suetonius, Domitian had made the children of his cousin Flavius Clemens his heirs, but had then had him executed and this – in some obscure way – triggered the plot. Struggles over the succession were bitter enough. There were stories that Claudius had been killed to ensure the succession of Nero, the son of his third wife, rather than Britannicus, who was the son of Messalina. The truth is that we have no knowledge of why Domitian was killed, just a sense of who rejoiced and who benefited.

By the time Suetonius and Dio wrote, a mass of omens, dreams and prophesies had of course accumulated around the murder, Nerva's succession and Domitian's funeral. Among them were the warnings, mostly astrological, that Domitian had received and either ignored or failed to respond to, but also miraculous announcements of his death, his abandonment by Minerva and the oracle of Fortuna at Praeneste, and a variety of utterances of Domitian made in his last days alive that turned out to have had sinister significance. The accumulated portents made his death seem timely, necessary and preordained. This much at least had not changed since the Ides of March.

⧗

The emperor was always a target, and no one was so close to him that he or she could be trusted without question. Death usually came from within the claustrophic world of the court. An ABC of assassination can easily be drawn up.

And the best guess in the imperial game of Cluedo? 'I accuse the praetorian guard, in the palace, with the dagger!'

First, the means. Poison was often suspected or alleged. Claudius's mushrooms were so notorious that an actor in Nero's day mimed eating them when the line 'Farewell father!' was read out. Rumours claimed that Tiberius was the victim of a slow-acting poison administered by Caligula. Caligula's father, the imperial prince Germanicus, was believed by some to have been poisoned, and Suetonius tells a story that Caligula excused his execution of his young cousin Tiberius Gemellus by saying that he smelled as if he had taken an antidote. Both Caligula and Nero were said to have kept boxes of poison. By Claudius's reign at least emperors provided themselves with tasters. But poison was unsure, it might be protected against or discovered, and it was often slow to act, a danger when every emperor was surrounded by doctors. So the most common of all weapons was the assassin's dagger. Getting one close to the emperor was the most difficult part. The ex-slave Stephanus, Domitian's killer, concealed a dagger in bandages wrapped around a fake wound on his arm. Barbers were particularly feared, since they had the licence to hold a blade to the emperor's throat. When Trajan wanted to demonstrate his trust of his lieutenant Licinius Sura he dismissed his bodyguard and had himself shaved by Sura's barber. Commodus reputedly singed his own hair with hot coals because he was afraid of barbers. It did not save him from strangulation by his personal trainer. Emperors themselves kept weapons around them. Domitian slept with a dagger under his pillow: but its blade was secretly removed before his murder.

Second, the perpetrators. The assassins themselves were for the most part imperial ex-slaves or members of the bodyguard. There was no easy defence against a conspiracy of bodyguards and servants of the bedchamber. Tiberius was in some accounts killed by the praetorian prefect Macro himself. Caligula was killed by a military tribune of the guard according to a plot that had originated with senators, commanders of the guard and imperial freedmen.

The emperors surrounded themselves with a variety of bodyguards. Most prominent were the praetorian guard, formed from the bodyguards that all great republican generals had organised, brigaded together from the reign of Tiberius in a great camp dominating the city, the traces of which survive today alongside Stazione Termini, the main railway station of Rome. Other units included German cavalrymen, urban cohorts and nightwatchmen who doubled as a fire brigade of sorts. Under Augustus there were maybe 7–8,000 troops in Rome. The number rose rapidly, reaching around 30,000 by the end of the second century. Guards were paid at rates high above those of ordinary soldiers, and their commanders, although not chosen from the senate, were among the most powerful figures after the emperor. When emperors travelled outside the city they were always accompanied by detachments of the guard. Tiberius's praetorian prefect Sejanus ruled Rome as a viceroy during the years of the emperor's self-imposed retreat to Capri. The guard was disbanded by Constantine in 312, but by then its commanders headed the imperial bureaucracy, and the Christian empire was divided into four great praetorian prefectures. Consuls and other senators were completely eclipsed by their power.

Alongside the soldiers there were the growing ranks of imperial slaves and ex-slaves (or freedmen), known as Caesar's household, the *familia Caesaris*. On Augustus's

death, he left the senate a short account of the current locations of the legions and the state of the imperial finances,
adding the names of the slaves and ex-slaves who could
supply further information. Just as the personal servants of
medieval kings became the chamberlains and chancellors of
state, so imperial servants of the bedchambers – the *cubicu-
larii* – and in their turn eunuch attendants came to control
access to the emperor. They were not only dependable but
also disposable servants. Deposing a consul was a scandal.
Relegating a great freedman or an equestrian prefect was
quite another matter. Dio tells the story of Commodus's
cubicularius Cleander. Allegedly he had come to Rome in
chains as a slave labourer but in the imperial household
rose to great power, marrying the emperor's concubine and
engineering the fall of the praetorian prefect Perennis, accusing him of plotting against the emperor. After Perennis's
fall Cleander was Commodus's confidant and enriched
himself selling positions in the senate and even consulships,
to aristocrats of course. His own downfall came when he
was blamed for a food crisis, one that Dio says was exacer-
bated by the equestrian prefect of the grain supply in order
to discredit Cleander. As an angry mob surged through the
city looking for the emperor, he was persuaded to sacrifice
Cleander to them by his concubine Marcia (who would
eventually be behind the plot that led to his own murder).
Imperial freedmen and equestrian prefects played a role that
has been observed in many other early empires, that of the
lightning conductor which can divert hostility away from an
emperor's person.

That at least was the theory. Of course the knowledge
that they were all potentially expendable made the loyalty
of every Lord High Substitute conditional. This applied

equally to those with less formal, but even more formidable, influence – the concubines like Marcia and their male counterparts. The final ingredient in the cocktail was the emperor's relatives, especially those women whose power depended on the favour given to their husbands and children. As emperors aged, or tired of their wives or partners, or shifted their affections among potential heirs, so great courtiers naturally wondered how to preserve their influence. From these circles conspiracies emerged. Of course they chose others to commit the deed itself. These lowly assassins could be fall guys too if a plot went wrong. The hero of Josephus's account of Caligula's murder is Chaerea, a lowly but noble-spirited member of Caligula's guard sickened by the atrocities he has to carry out as well as enraged by the emperor's mockery of him. He stiffens the sinews of his senatorial backers, co-ordinates the coup and carries out the murder with his fellow guardsmen in one of the narrow passages that wind between the various imperial houses on the Palatine. It is he and other lowly figures who protect the senators when Caligula's German bodyguard runs amok, but when the praetorians declare Claudius emperor, the senate – which had been debating the restoration of Liberty – agree to Chaerea's execution. The praetorians themselves were behind many successful plots. Their access to the emperor above all determined this. And a few emperors struck the fatal blow themselves. No one could order an emperor to commit suicide, but two emperors who had lost everything did just this, Nero and later his one-time friend Otho.

Third, the time and place. The ideal occasion would be a public one, like that chosen for the death of Caesar. Killing an emperor in private carried the risk that some would believe he still lived. A series of 'False Neros' appeared in

14/15/16/17
Four faces of Roman tyranny, clockwise from top left: mad Caligula slain by his guards; sinister Commodus strangled by his personal trainer; Maximinus Thrax, first of a line of brutal soldier-emperors feared and loathed by the senate; Elagabalus, whose exotic religious and sexual tastes embarrassed and unnerved Rome. All are, of course, memorialised by their enemies.

the years following his suicide, to cause minor annoyance to his Flavian successors. Proof was generally needed. When Avidius Cassius's rebellion failed, his head was brought to Marcus Aurelius to demonstrate his death. But the obstacles to a public assassination were immense. Even when the assassin was a member of his bodyguard, the others were not always in on the plan. In the chaos that surrounded a public assassination there was likely to be indiscriminate bloodshed. Besides, on public occasions the emperors took special precautions. Suetonius wrote that Augustus once wore a sword and breastplate under his tunic when he addressed the senate. He also reported, citing Cremutius Cordus, that no senator was allowed to approach Augustus until he had been searched for daggers. Dio claimed Augustus habitually wore armour under his robes in the senate. Cicero too had worn a breastplate below his toga during the Catiline conspiracy. Julius Caesar had neglected these elementary precautions on the Ides of March. So the typical assassination was a hurried attack when the emperor was off his guard. Caligula was attacked during the Palatine games. Caracalla was murdered in the Syrian desert by a group of his bodyguards when he had dismounted to relieve himself. Commodus was killed while exercising.

The best place to kill an emperor was where he felt safest, in the palace. Augustus had taken up residence on the exclusive Palatine Hill between the forum and the Circus Maximus, and his family gradually took over all the residential property on the hill, turning it into a maze of separate houses, interspersed with temples and open spaces. Gradually grander structures emerged incorporating great dining complexes, gardens, state rooms, shrines, offices of state, slave quarters, grand kitchens, bath complexes and the private quarters of the imperial family. Monumental approaches led down to the forum and, eventually, opened out over the Circus, where later emperors met their people. Caligula died in the maze of alleys that separated the houses of the first century Palatine. Later emperors were more likely to meet their assassins in the inner quarters, the bedroom above all, but also in dining areas or even the baths. Heavy security surrounded the palace and protected the emperors from maniacs or enraged private citizens. It also ensured that most were murdered by those they knew well and trusted.

Finally, the news had to be announced, a shape put around the events. After Commodus's death the senate issued a jubilant proclamation.

> May all honours be stripped from this enemy of his fatherland! May all honours be stripped from this parricide. Drag away this murderer. Let this public enemy, this butcher, this gladiator be thrown in the dust. He was an enemy of the gods, a slaughterer of the senate, an enemy of the gods, a murderer of the senate, he was an enemy of the gods, an enemy of the senate. Throw the gladiator in the dirt, let the man who murdered the senate be thrown down, let his body be dragged on a hook, let the man who murdered the innocent be dragged on a hook. Enemy, parricide, truly, truly.

And so it continues, until the abuse of Commodus merges into praise of his successor Pertinax and cries of long life to the praetorian guard and to the army. The senate had played no part in Commodus's removal, which had been plotted by the praetorian prefect Laetus and Marcia, the emperor's concubine. Nor did the senate choose Pertinax, who had been more or less compelled to present himself to the praetorians with all the usual promises of cash. But the senate celebrated their day of freedom, declaring the destruction of Commodus's statues, listing his crimes, branding him more cruel than Domitian and more defiled than Nero.

Senators themselves never emerge well from these stories. Often we find them gloating over the death of a prince, desecrating his memory and then flattering his successor in the terms they had used, only days before, to the murdered 'tyrant'. Informers were routinely vilified in the abstract, but when an emperor died those senators he had promoted often moved effortlessly into the friendship of his replacement. Frequently, the senate appear terrified of the people and of the guard. If some accounts make this an occasion to condemn the lower classes for subservience, others imply that some emperors were only tyrants in the eyes of their aristocratic subjects, perhaps not even in the eyes of the senate as a whole. Even at the moment of freedom, when on Caligula's death some senators felt the chance had come to restore the republic, others were jockeying for the position of emperor. Nor was the senate averse to tyrannical atrocities of its own. One of its first acts was to send a guardsman to murder Caligula's widow and their eighteen-month-old daughter. When Tiberius's praetorian prefect Sejanus fell from grace his family too had been murdered on the senate's authority: his daughter was raped first, to avoid the pollution that might come from killing a virgin. The families of Perennis and of Cleander also perished in their respective falls from grace. All these innocent victims were well known to the senators, indeed many of them were their friends and relatives.

On Pertinax's accession all Commodus's own concessions to the guard were confirmed. The emperor's body was given funeral honours at Pertinax's orders. The organisers of the coup, Laetus and Marcia, continued in their positions of influence. Pertinax's resistance to the senate's protests did not ensure the loyalty of Laetus, who soon engineered another assassination, again by guardsmen. The next emperor, Didius Julianus, was also put in power by the praetorians, at the price of another gift and the promise to restore Commodus's good name.

⧗

Assassination attempts and palace conspiracies have loomed over many monarchies and empires. Given the powerful forces that generated successive murders and plots in Rome, it is almost worth asking whether Rome was special. Did monarchy and conspiracy keep company in all pre-modern empires? The answer seems to be that, although many of the same dynamics can be found in other empires, not all pre-industrial rulers were quite so liable as the Caesars to be murdered by their entourages.

Ottoman politics, for instance, during the fifteenth and sixteenth centuries was far from tranquil. There are many instances of civil war, riots and struggles for office and favour at court. But most sultans do not seem to have gone in such fear of their lives. Like the Roman emperors, the Ottomans in some senses owned their servants, but they succeeded in binding them more closely to the Sublime Porte. Many devices were used to achieve this end. Grand viziers were in some periods married to female relatives of the sultan. Nothing quite like the senate existed as focus for discontent. For most of the imperial period, the sultans neither married nor slept with the daughters of the aristocracy: their celibate marriages were contracted with foreigners and their children fathered on concubines. These were kept in seclusion until each bore a male child, at which point she raised him separately. Alliances between aristocrats, imperial slaves and concubines that formed the basis of so many Roman plots would have been much more difficult to engineer. There were more ferocious devices too. Torture was widely used to cow even courtiers. And although the hereditary principle was adhered to strictly, there was no preference for the eldest son. Successions always involved political manoeuvring and sometimes pitched battles: when a new sultan did accede he was expected to have all his brothers executed. But although this brutal regime terrified many future sultans, few were murdered once in power. Intrigues did take place, and increasingly a key role was played by the Janissaries, the elite guard recruited from subject peoples and raised from boyhood in the sultan's service. But their objectives were not always assassination. Mehmed II, Bayezid II and Mustafa I were all forced to abdicate. Other sultans were merely compelled to give up unpopular policies or, like Commodus, surrender unpopular ministers to be killed. When Osman II was murdered in a Janissary rebellion, the act caused real horror among the Janissaries as well as more widely. The deposition and execution of Ibrahim in 1648 came only after years of madness and at the height of a major military and political crisis.

One question to ponder is why Roman emperors were never deposed rather than killed? During the Byzantine middle ages a succession of emperors was removed, and their return to power prevented by blinding and sometimes castrating them or by compelling them to take holy orders.

Michael Psellus's series of imperial lives, which in some ways resembles those of Suetonius or the Augustan *History*, catalogues a grim succession of forced abdications. Only once, during the horrors of the Fourth Crusade, was a blind emperor recalled to the throne. The origin of the idea that a maimed man could not be emperor is difficult to track down. It is certainly not Roman, or else the crippled Claudius could never have been imposed by the praetorians. The apparent madness of Caligula or Elagabal – who allegedly appointed a favourite dancer to command of the guard and turned the palace into a public bath – would have resulted in deposition in the Ottoman empire rather than their murder. Did Romans have no means of making men ineligible for rule? Or was it simply that medieval Christian and Islamic states were less willing than Romans to contemplate tyrannicide? Few kings were killed deliberately in western Christendom, although many were imprisoned or otherwise controlled.

Did religion protect kings and emperors from the assassin's knife? This question is less easy to answer than it seems. Certainly one or other version of divine sanction was common, indeed almost universal, in ancient empires. The Ottoman sultan styled himself the shadow of God on earth, Merovingian kings were anointed, the church played a role in the coronation of many medieval monarchs and the German emperors. The Chinese emperors were Sons of Heaven, and their religious authority long pre-dated the establishment of a political system or military supremacy. The pharaohs were living gods and so were the Inka. Individual rulers often tried to harness a new cult to enhance their legitimacy: the most famous include Akhenaten's experiments with monotheism in Egypt, Asoka's with Buddhism in India, and Constantine's with Christianity in the Roman world. The Persian kings of the Achaemenid dynasty marshalled support from all sides – Marduk in Babylon, Apollo in Greek Asia Minor, the God of the Jews in Jerusalem as well as Ahura Mazda, their ancestral god of light. The cult paid by subjects to their kings and the prayers made on their behalf are increasingly seen as ways in which the enormous power of emperors could be accommodated within traditional religious systems. Monarchs and emperors too needed to find some relationship between their power and the cosmic order.

Strangely, these ritual exchanges between ruler and subject offered little protection against the assassin's knife. Like Hellenistic kings before them, the Roman emperors received a variety of kinds of ruler cult. They were pharaohs in Egypt, god-like mortals who shared the temples of the Gods in the Greek world, worshipped as living gods by many of their inhabitants. Romans worshipped those deceased emperors who had been deified by senatorial decree, sacrificed to the living emperor's *genius* or spirit, and dedicated altars 'In Honour of the Divine House'. Jews and Christians – some of them – claimed that although they would not worship the Caesars they would pray on their behalf. And yet assassination continued. It was the same in many other early empires. Some Muslim writers believed that a successful revolt manifested the will of God, that God raised up usurpers against unjust rulers. Max Weber called this the 'theodicy of good fortune', the idea that success in obtaining and maintaining power is demonstration enough of divine favour, of what the Chinese termed 'the mandate of heaven'. The Roman senate deified only Good Emperors, at least in theory: in practice the views of the next emperor were paramount.

Perhaps more powerful protection against assassination was given by strict laws of succession. Many medieval

European monarchs came to be locked into terrible conflicts with their elder sons, some of whom gathered a sort of second court around them. But when succession was so strongly conditioned by a belief in the importance of primogeniture there was never any scope for plots designed to advance one potential heir at the expense of another. Nero could never have succeeded a medieval Claudius in place of Britannicus, and a medieval Augustus could never have wavered over the rival merits of his grandsons and his stepchildren. Equally, sons and fathers were drawn back together by a common interest in the preservation of the patrimony. Conflict was diverted, of course, rather than avoided. Romans worried much less about the legitimacy of their children than did medieval monarchs. Roman emperors were accused of sleeping with their sisters and nieces, but not of being bastards. And when the choice of heirs was small, the emperor's sons did sometimes behave with the arrogance and glamour of medieval Young Kings and Crown Princes. Both Titus and Domitian enjoyed to the full the sensual opportunities offered them as emperors-in-waiting. Although some second-century emperors were praised for selecting the best of possible heirs from the senate, no emperor ever preferred a non-relative over his own son. Most were aware that a clear line of succession deterred many assassins.

Machiavelli, who thought that plots against princes were inevitable, pointed out that the Roman emperors were unlucky in that while most princes had to contend with the ambition of the nobles and the insolence of the people, they also had to face the cruelty and greed of the soldiery. We might add other contingent factors of a sociological nature. The Roman court was closer to the aristocracy than many of its counterparts: the emperors were not quite so remote, so clearly separate by blood or divine ancestry. The slow institutionalisation of the Roman court society cannot have helped. The ground rules for Roman monarchy were laid down by Augustus, who well remembered the Ides of March. The power of the guard and the absence of clear rules of succession of the kind enjoyed by overt monarchies were both arguably part of Augustus's reaction to Julius Caesar's murder. So was a senate that knew how to tell the difference between a tyrant and a king and revered tyrannicides. Founded in Julius Caesar's blood, the early empire was doomed to relive his murder again and again.

As a matter of fact, there were some Roman thinkers who had reached a similar analysis, or at least who had concluded, like Machiavelli, that assassination was intrinsic to the imperial monarchy. Seneca describes how the merciful prince inspires such great affection when his subjects know he has their interests at heart that they protect him against all comers.

> They are ready to throw themselves on the daggers of his assailants and lay down their lives for him, if his path to safety must be across their slaughtered bodies.

Behind the hyperbolic expression of the old trope that the king is the head to the people's body lies the assumption that even the best of emperors will face assassins.

But there is an even more interesting set of discussions embedded in Cassius Dio's account of the reign of Augustus. A Greek intellectual and a Roman senator, he was close enough to the imperial court to witness at first hand the alternation of tyranny and order between the reigns of Commodus and Severus Alexander. That period included the assassinations of Commodus, Pertinax, Didius Julianus, Geta, Caracalla, Opellius Macarinus and Elagabal, and the Severan civil war which resulted in the deaths of the two pretenders, Pescennius Niger and Clodius Albinus. Dio was the consummate senatorial survivor. He rose to power under Commodus, won the office of praetor under Pertinax, wrote a pamphlet describing the dreams that predicted Severus's accession and later presented Severus with a history of the civil wars through which he achieved it. Dio was consul under Severus and accompanied the court of his son Caracalla to the east. Legionary commands and a prestigious governorship followed, and in 229 he had the honour of sharing his second consulship with the new emperor, Alexander Severus. His history of Rome from the beginning to his own day was written over twelve years in the middle of his career.

Dio had no illusions about the reality of tyranny. One personal anecdote describes how, sitting with fellow senators in the front row at the games, he chewed on leaves from his ceremonial wreath to avoid laughing at Commodus's antics in the arena when he played at being a gladiator. Being seen to ridicule the prince would certainly have meant death. Looking back over almost a thousand years of Roman history and two centuries of the imperial monarchy, Dio was also able to consider what kind of state Rome had become and why. Like his stylistic model, Thucydides, Dio was interested in the constants of history, in the institutions and structures that reasserted themselves again and again in the course of events. His attention was naturally transfixed by

Rome's reinvention as a monarchy, and he took time in his long account of Augustus's reign to examine the new cluster of institutions that emerged. Again like Thucydides, he reflected on these matters through speeches and debates put into the mouths of the key protagonists. Most famous is the debate he stages in Book 52 between Augustus's two closest advisers, Agrippa and Maecenas, on whether to restore the democracy (the republic that is) or whether to create a monarchy. The dramatic date is 29 BC, just after Octavian's victory was secured.

There was a long tradition of debates of this kind in Greek histories. Herodotus, the 'Father of History', himself began the tradition with the story, certainly false, of a discussion between three Persian noblemen who had just effected a coup d'état over whether their empire should become a democracy, an oligarchy or a monarchy. Thucydides was the master of these set-pieces: the tale of the fall of the Athenian empire gave no opportunity for overt discussion of the merits of democracy, but there are many opportunities to comment on the subject. One speaker tells the massed Athenians that theirs is a tyrant city, ruling over other cities as a tyrant rules over his subjects. So much for a democracy founded in tyrannicide! Dio returns to all these themes in his great debate. Agrippa argues for the restoration of democracy in Rome, pointing out the evils that come from tyranny and the difficulty monarchs have in avoiding it. Maecenas, like his Persian prototype, argues that having won power it would be dangerous to try to give it up and that democracy too is flawed, the people are irresponsible and only a strong hand can effectively guide the Roman state.

But Dio is interested in much more than recapitulating this old sophistic contest over the respective merits of different constitutions. Maecenas goes on to offer Augustus, the silent audience, a blueprint of the imperial state as it actually emerged, arguing for passing laws through the senate, for making use of equestrians as salaried officials, for instituting a standing army, for generous enfranchisement and so on. Augustus, at the end of the speech, not only accepts Maecenas's advice over Agrippa's. He decides to implement only some of Maecenas's ideas at once, introducing others later and even leaving some for his successors. The Roman imperial system, in reality an ever-changing product of experimentation and short-term expediency like any other government, is presented as the product of a coherent plan, providentially predicted on the first day of empire, but brought into being in phases following an ancient design. If, as is likely, part of this was performed to Caracalla and his court as it toured Asia Minor, the conceit would have delighted the emperor not only in its deft application of classical models to Roman history, but also in the pattern it discerned in the past. The theodicy, again, of good fortune. Dio's own foresight did not let him down. He had left the court and returned to Rome well before Caracalla's own murder in the Syrian desert.

Where does assassination figure in Maecenas's speech? Like Seneca he takes for granted that there will be plots aimed against Augustus and every emperor. Senators and their relatives, if accused of plotting, should be tried by their peers so that the ill-feeling aroused by the exile or death of the guilty should be borne by the senate, not the emperor. Augustus should be lenient with those who insulted him, and should treat convicted plotters with clemency.

And if anyone is accused of conspiring against you – for

such a thing may indeed come about – avoid being his judge yourself, or prejudging the case, since it is not appropriate that the same person should be both prosecutor and juror, but bring him before the senate and let him defend himself there and if he is convicted, be moderate in deciding his punishment *so that everyone will believe he is really guilty.* For most people find it really hard to believe that someone without weapons would plot against someone who is armed. The only way to persuade them is this, to fix a penalty that does not seem to derive from anger or a desire to make an example of him. The only exception to this rule is when someone raises an army and revolts openly. For someone like that ought not to be tried at all, but rather punished as an enemy.

Dio even gives Augustus a chance to apply this advice towards the end of his life when the conspiracy of Cinna is revealed to him. Augustus is presented with a dilemma. Execution or forgiveness seemed equally likely to provoke further dissent. This time it is not Maecenas but the empress Livia who counsels mercy:

It is no surprise that men plot against you, indeed it is human nature that they do. Ruling an empire as large as yours you are bound to do many things which naturally upset many people. No ruler can please everyone in all things. Even a ruler who is entirely just must of necessity make many enemies.

Livia goes on to argue that not only criminals but even those ambitious to achieve great honour will be among his enemies. Not only will Augustus have personal enemies:

some will attack him simply because he is monarch. Envy and treachery can be counted on. Augustus's best defence is to defend his position strenuously. For this he needs the army, a bodyguard.

> Then Augustus replied, 'I hardly need to say that many men have on many occasions perished at the hands of those closest to them. Even more than for other people this is true of monarchies, that we need to fear not only our enemies but also our friends. After all, more monarchs have been plotted against by those who are around them all the time, day and night, when they are exercising and when they are eating and drinking, than have been threatened by strangers. Against strangers we may deploy our friends, but against our friends there is no one we can trust as an ally.

Augustus expands on the theme and Livia agrees, but then tentatively she offers her final advice, that Augustus should exercise mercy. Philanthropia – a kind generosity of spirit – is the emperor's best defence. Forgiveness breeds gratitude and admiration, while harshness will only inspire more plots. Her speech is a long one, and recapitulates all those arguments that Seneca, and before him Cicero, found in those Hellenistic Greek treatises *On Kingship*, and that had been used again by another Bithynian Dio in Trajan's reign and by Pliny in his *Panegyric*. As long as kings – Greek or Roman – dominated the political life of the Mediterranean there would be audiences for speeches that counselled princes to use their absolute power with restraint, to temper justice with mercy. Cassius Dio, a senator himself, had his own interest in dissuading princes from tyranny. Whether or not he could truly have believed that kindness would ward off the assassins' knife is more dubious. More likely he too had concluded that even the best of emperors would face attempts on his life. The advice not to respond with savage retribution might prevent failed plots from driving emperors into tyranny. Dio must have known too that not all plots would fail.

Yet Brutus and Cassius and Cato were still celebrated, symbols of the stern morality of the republic and of a refusal to compromise with tyranny. Wise emperors tolerated this postering by senatorial intellectuals, choosing to hear in the criticism of tyranny no attack on their own unimpeachable reigns. Caesar had dissented from the eulogies of Cato written by Cicero and Brutus, but politely. Augustus took care to praise Cicero, and although he called the historian Livy a follower of Pompey he carefully did not complain. But during the reign of Tiberius, the senator Cremutius Cordus was accused of treason because in his histories he had praised Brutus and called Cassius 'the last of the Romans'. Tacitus gives him a long speech in which he complains that Livy had celebrated Pompey without it harming his friendship with Augustus, and had never referred to any of the Pompeians or to Brutus or Cassius as 'bandits and murderers' as was now the custom. Asinius Pollio and Messala Corvinus had even praised them. Cordus was sentenced to suicide all the same, and the senate ordered that his books be burned. Ben Jonson reworked these passages in his *Sejanus*. Throughout the first century they remained symbols of resistance. A life of Cato was written by Thrasea Paetus, one of a group of senators who in Nero's reign shared Seneca's interests in Stoicism, but made it a vehicle for criticising the regime. Seneca too wrote in admiration of Cato, but without any sense of support for republicanism. Lucan's epic poem on the civil war between Caesar and Pompey is the only work of this kind that survives. Caesar is a tyrant, whose very mercy marks out his monarchical aspirations. Cato is the doomed defender of liberty, Brutus the last hope of freedom. The poem was linked with Lucan's fall from favour in Nero's court and the order that he commit suicide. Tacitus's *Dialogue on Oratory*, which has a dramatic date of AD 75, opens with two orators visiting a third, Curiatus Maternus, who the day before had given a performance of a tragedy entitled the *Cato* in which Caesar's enemy was idolised. When his visitors protest that this sort of writing is dangerous – it had offended some of the powerful, presumably at court – Maternus is defiant, and promises a sequel. But by Tacitus's own day the emperors were evidently more tolerant.

Pliny the Younger celebrates the knight Titinius Capito for obtaining permission from Trajan to set up a statue to one of Nero's victims, Lucius Silanus. The episode is made to reflect well on Trajan's liberality and Capito's virtue in not forgetting what he owes to his friend, and Pliny elaborates the theme, pointing out how Capito's action will win him future praise (and by implication Pliny's memorialising of Capito will do the same for him). That notion of fame accumulating through acts of remembering is a theme close to Pliny's heart. For those many Romans who believed in no afterlife, this sort of posterity was intensely important. Eulogies like those that Cicero and Brutus wrote of Cato, or like the one Tacitus wrote of his father-in-law Agricola, took their place alongside tombs, statues and inscriptions in preserving the memory of the deeds and qualities of the noble dead. Destruction of images and the obliteration of names – the treatment handed out to Sejanus, Domitian and Commodus – was the flip side of this coin. The statue to Silanus, Pliny goes on, is no isolated instance of Capito's care that the virtuous be remembered.

> It is just like Capito, who makes a habit of revering famous men. Most impressive is the care he takes for the bust of Brutus, Cassius and Cato which he has set up at home wherever he can. He also commemorates the lives of the greatest men in excellent verse.

The tyrannicides have joined the ranks of virtuous Romans, enemies not of the Caesars so much as of vice, appropriately revered in an age in which Pliny can sing the royal virtues of an emperor, and in which Tacitus can proclaim the reconciliation of liberty and imperial Rome. Both, of course, remembered the tyranny of Domitian and his assassination and neither was under any illusions that many more tyrants and assassinations lay ahead. For them, as for Dio, the alternation of tyranny and kingship had come to seem the Roman way.

4

AFTERSHOCKS

Caesar's murder has reverberated down through history. This is so obvious that it no longer surprises, but it should. Why should one murdered politician matter after all this time? Even in classical antiquity he was not the first tyrant to be slain, nor the last. Murders are excellent punctuation marks to be sure. The deaths of Charles I, the princes in the tower, the Archduke Franz Ferdinand, Trotsky and the icepick all resonate. Narratives of monarchies hardly ever resist using the deaths and accession of kings to provide chapter headings. But among so many murdered and perished leaders of men, why do the Ides of March still matter? The aftershocks of Caesar's murder make sense only as part of the seismology of antiquity in the contemporary world.

Caesar's murder entered casually into the cultural bloodstream of Europe from the Renaissance. It became immediately a part of popular as well as elite culture, a convenient symbol, easily understood. From the eighteenth century on the names Cato, Brutus and Cassius evoked immediate recognition, and sporadic adulation. They came with certain fixed connotations, of course (hence their utility), but they were also plastic, and easier to manipulate than biblical texts or topical gossip. Antiquity sanitised these violent events, and lent them a kind of grandeur. No one was any longer

Brutus's descendant, nor Caesar's. Ancient Rome was far away in time and space. The Ides of March became, in Claude Lévi-Strauss's phrase, 'good to think with'. So they remain today.

The routes by which key moments of classical history escaped the great forgetting that followed the catastrophe of the ancient world were very various. Libraries burned or simply rotted when the aristocracies that had tended them were replaced by Christian bishops and barbarian kings. For a moment like the Ides of March to survive, it had to be captured in the amber of a classical text. That text then had to survive either in the libraries of Byzantium or the monastic *scriptoria* of the West (and sometimes only in translation into Arabic, Syriac or Armenian). Finally, it had to be recovered, edited, copied, publicised and printed to ensure survival. Each route to modernity was a little different, and following any single one is the work of a detective or an archaeologist.

Caesar's posterity is so vast, and some parts of it – Shakespeare's play above all – so overwhelming in their cultural impact, that a direct approach might easily yield an unwieldy list of attestations and references, allusions and imitations, casual mimicry and vivid re-enactments of the Ides of March. And it is slaughtered Caesar that concerns us, not Caesar the conqueror, Caesar the demagogue or imperial Caesars of the kind that have exercised such various fascinations. So I shall sneak up on Caesar, as it were, by beginning with another player in the drama, but one just as vital in the post-classical debates on tyranny and its cure. Dead long before the Ides of March, and by his own hand rather than an assassin's, Cato the Younger nevertheless haunted Caesar's brief dictatorship. His choice – to die rather than look on tyranny – was immediately the subject of controversy. His is the silent voice in the agonising of the conspirators before the Ides of March. His death would be a model for that of his son-in-law Brutus. And under imperial tyrannies, Cato was celebrated, alongside Brutus and Cassius, as one of the last martyrs of the republic. Lucan, opening the epic poem of the civil war he began under Nero and did not complete before he too perished in a failed conspiracy, asks whether Pompey or Caesar had the better cause to take up arms.

> We may not know the answer, for each side had mighty support
> The gods preferred the victorious cause, but Cato the defeated one.

No mandate of heaven for Lucan, and self-murdered Cato rivalled assassinated Caesar in their intermingled afterlives.

⧗

Cato was thoroughly mythologised within months of his death, especially among the circle of those who knew him best. None of the pamphlets written and politely circulated in the months before Caesar's murder survived. They were handwritten, of course, and few copies ever existed. But they gathered up a mass of good and bad opinions and some splendid anecdotes that did survive. Cato was an awkward character, surly and relatively friendless, a workaholic by day who relaxed in all-night drinking sessions with philosophers.

He was perhaps respected more than he was liked. During the civil war he twice survived military defeats because he had been left in charge of a fortified post. Was his stern and uncompromising advice not always welcome on the battlefield? There was probably no politician in Rome whose nose he did not get up on one occasion or another. Caesar once jailed him for obstructing his plans. At one point, Cato's enemies managed to get him posted to a dead-end position in Cyprus. Of course he turned it to his advantage and won great public acclaim for his probity and diligence. But touring through Asia, he not only refused all the presents offered him by local dynasts but he also refused to let any of his retinue accept them. He never made it to the consulship. But he had a noble name and most importantly was a ferocious orator. Plutarch, whose *Life of Cato the Younger* is the main source for most of the stories, says he could talk all day in a debate if necessary. Like any moralist he attracted stories of inconsistent behaviour. Even Plutarch seems shocked at the story of how Cato divorced his wife so she could marry one of his friends and give him children, and then remarried her when she had done just this. Cato features in a few of the speeches and letters of Cicero. The two were politically allied on numerous occasions: both were committed to defending the prerogatives of the senate against the generals, and neither had much time for the popular party. But they were not close. Cicero's encomium of Cato is lost, but he is mentioned several times in the works that Cicero composed during and after Caesar's dictatorship. Cicero praised Cato as the perfect Stoic and as a man of virtue, and he defended his decision to die in *On Duties*. The suspicion remains that he found Cato easier to deal with dead than alive. Cato wrote nothing himself. Only the speeches he gave during the conspiracy of Catiline in 63 were recorded, and then only because Cicero had brought shorthand writers into the debate. Sallust gives Cato a speech in this debate, in which he opposed Caesar's proposal that the accused conspirators should be simply imprisoned. Cato supported – successfully – Cicero's proposal that they be executed without trial. Perhaps Sallust had read Cato's actual words, but we cannot know for sure, and the sort of speech inserted into a history was always far shorter than the real thing.

Cato survives then not in his own words, but as a character described by others. Of all his notable deeds, the one that defines him is his suicide in the north African town of Utica on hearing the news of Caesar's victory at nearby Thapsus. For many he became quite simply Cato Uticensis, Cato of Utica. Caesar is said to have reproached his corpse for having robbed him of the chance of sparing his life. That was the whole point. Cato, it would be said, preferred an honourable death to living without liberty. He could have fled to Spain where Pompey's sons still led the resistance. He could conceivably have remained in the senate until Caesar was forced to silence him. He might have gone into ostentatious self-imposed exile as Cicero did. But suicide suited Cato. It was, in any case, an acceptable option in Rome. When it resulted from a free choice made rationally and carried out calmly, suicide might signify fortitude and philosophical detachment. Cato's choice not only accused Caesar of tyranny. It also reproached those followers of Pompey who had elected to accept the dictator's clemency, men like Cicero, Brutus and Cassius. As in his life, so in his death Cato would not give up the competition for the reputation of most moral of the Romans. No wonder his death aroused such strong feelings.

Not just feelings, of course, but words. The pamphlets were only the beginning. The events of the civil war inspired a mass of memoirs. Among others, we know of accounts by Cato's friend Munatius Rufus, by Brutus's stepson and by his friend Volumnius, and by Quintus Dellius, who swapped allegiance back and forth throughout the wars. All but fragments are now lost, but they were used by the first generation of historians to try to make sense of the civil wars. Sallust's histories dealt with the seventies and sixties and Asinius Pollio wrote a detailed history of the fifties and forties. Cremutius Cordus's history survived the Tiberian book-burning, at least in part. Plutarch had access to most of it and also to the work of the next generation of writers, including Thrasea's *Life of Cato* (based, says Plutarch, mostly on Munatius Plancus's account) and odd reminiscences in the encyclopedia of Pliny the Elder. Finally there is Plutarch's biography of Cato, the major surviving source for his life and death, part of that great collection of *Parallel Lives* in which biographies of great figures from classical Greece were paired with those of Roman republican heroes, and compared in terms of their moral character and development.

Plutarch had already written *Lives* of Lucullus and Cicero when he wrote the *Cato*. About the same time he was also writing lives of Pompey, Caesar, Brutus, Crassus and Antony. All are extensive and very detailed, and testify to the amount of material available. But it was not only facts about Cato that existed in abundance. A fully formed image of Cato had already been created, one that was essentially the same, in a wide range of texts. Already by Augustus's reign, Cato had become a conventional figure for unconquerable virtue. The poets Horace and Virgil celebrated his intransigence, the historians Livy and Velleius Paterculus seem to have done the same, and he is already an archetype in the works for orators produced by Valerius Maximus and Seneca the Elder. Virgil and the astronomer-poet Manilius even imagine honourable afterlives for Cato. The former pictured him giving justice in the underworld, a stern and civilising influence among the dead in succession to the law-givers of Greek Hades, Minos and Rhadamanthus. Manilius described Cato dwelling with the souls of other heroes in the Milky Way. Cato was heroised by the Stoic writers of Nero's reign, Seneca the Younger and Lucan, as well as Thrasea. But the influence of the philosophers was not as long-lasting as that of the orators. The Greek historians Appian and Dio too produced accounts of Cato's death, but neither was as vivid or memorable as Plutarch's. When the name of Cato occurs in later antiquity, in the works of Macrobius, Jerome, Lactantius and Augustine among others, it refers to the stock *exemplum* he had become, the noble suicide who chose death over slavery.

Plutarch's biography draws on all this, and shows strong traces of the encomia with which Romans celebrated the noble dead. Perhaps the tributes penned by Cicero and Brutus had already determined the form in which Cato would be remembered. In any case, Cato's death scene is highly dramatised and the undoubted climax of Plutarch's work. Cato reads and re-reads Plato's *Phaedo*, debates the afterlife with his intimates in the manner of Socrates, and despite their pleading and attempts to obstruct him throws himself on his sword. Following his example, other senators sought Socratic deaths of this kind. Tacitus makes a kind of motif of these suicides in his account of Nero's reign, until it becomes what Barthes called a 'funerary baroque'. It is like a fugue in structure, each suicide offering a new variant on the Catonian and Socratic theme. Seneca surpasses himself (and

18. *Cato tears out his own entrails in Giovanni Battista's seventeenth century study based on Plutarch's vivid account of the suicide.*

Cato) in his calm imitation of Socrates. Petronius, Nero's 'connoisseur of elegance', goes out in style, substituting inconsequential chatter for sober philosophical discourse, and taste for morality. It is one of the greatest losses of classical literature that we do not possess the final suicide with which Tacitus must have closed the sequence, the spectacle of an emperor taking his own life, in a messy and botched and cowardly fashion. Plutarch's Cato does not in fact quite achieve Socratic composure or Senecan poise in his death. He is not especially calm. When a slave did not fetch him his sword, Cato hit him in the mouth so hard he hurt his own hand. At that point he lost his cool completely. His last moments are more worthy of Basil Fawlty than a Stoic sage. And, in a grotesque finale, Cato fights off a doctor who is trying to repair his wound, and then rips out his own entrails to be on the safe side. The story is one of several in Plutarch's account of Cato's career, in which excessive attention to his private virtue seems inappropriate for the statesman.

⧗

Plutarch's *Lives* were not the only vector through which Cato survived antiquity. Dante approached his Cato – a stern and rather unsympathetic guardian of Purgatory – through Cicero, Virgil and Lucan. But Cato's enormous success in the eighteenth century depended most of all on that of Plutarch, and so we now need to follow, for a little while, the relay race that carried Plutarch's work safely through the dark ages to the Enlightenment and beyond.

Plutarch's work was already a great success in his own lifetime. All his writings were philosophical in nature, but they wore his considerable learning lightly and were elegantly and entertainingly written. There were humorous pieces like a debate between Odysseus and one of his men, transformed into a pig by Circe, over whether humans or animals had a happier life. There were dialogues, and books of table-talk that imitated the learned conversation that readers imagined took place at philosophers' banquets. Essays dealt with topics of current fascination – Alexander the Great and the gods of the Egyptians, for example. And a number of his works dealt with the peculiarities of Roman culture, a subject of intensive interest to those educated Greeks who were just beginning to find places for themselves in the imperial hierarchy in Plutarch's lifetime. Most popular of all were the *Parallel Lives*.

Plutarch's works were read by Christian and pagan

writers alike into late antiquity. The growing popularity of Platonism may have helped, but there is a hint of a popular readership in Athens at least. The *Lives* posed few problems for Christian readers: Plutarch's heroes were characterised by self-control, by courage, by a broad education and an appreciation of Hellenic culture, his villains by the lack of all these things. His works were praised by Greek writers of the sixth century and survived the Byzantine Dark Ages to enjoy a burst of popularity in the eleventh and twelfth centuries. The great Byzantine scholar Maximus Planudes prepared an edition at the very end of the thirteenth century. A century later one copy at least had made its way west to a private library in Padua. A few manuscripts of the eleventh and twelfth centuries from French and Austrian monasteries show that some of the *Lives* at least had survived in the Latin west too. But it was not until copies of Byzantine texts were brought west that Plutarch took hold on a wider audience. They were much sought after by Italian buyers, to judge from the requests they made of their Greek suppliers. During the fourteenth century abbreviated versions of the *Lives* circulated in Greek, Aragonese and Tuscan dialects. The fifteenth century saw the first Latin translations. Some of the brightest stars of the Renaissance participated in the translation, among them Erasmus and Politian. The first Latin printed edition of the *Lives* was produced in 1470. From this point on they were accessible to a broad European intelligentsia, one that read Latin fluently but Greek hardly at all.

But the key breakthrough was into mass vernacular versions, into Italian, French, Spanish, German and English. Jacques Amyot's French version of the *Lives* was produced in 1559. Twenty years later an English translation of Amyot's was published by Thomas North. These translations and their successors had an enormous influence. Plutarch was suddenly one of the most accessible classical texts for a wide reading public. Read by Racine and Shakespeare, he inspired much classical drama in French and English. Plutarch remained ubiquitous throughout the seventeenth and eighteenth centuries. On both sides of the Atlantic the *Lives* were regarded as morally improving. Among those who claimed to have been educated in manners and morals by them were Benjamin Franklin and Frankenstein's Monster. The success of his *Lives* in early America has been well documented. The Greek text was barely studied in the classical curriculum, but in translation the *Lives* were one of the mostly widely read and owned classical works during the eighteenth century in colonial America. They feature in most private collections of colonial New England, and were commonly mentioned in the wills of middle-class families. And nestling in the heart of the *Lives,* among all those other improving examples, was that of Cato of Utica. It was in the eighteenth century that Cato enjoyed his most spectacular revival, on both sides of the Atlantic.

At the turn of the seventeenth and eighteenth centuries the Whig scholar and statesman Joseph Addison was privately at work on a tragedy, based on the life, or rather the death, of Cato. A new translation of the *Lives*, co-ordinated by John Dryden, had just appeared, giving them a new currency. But Addison cannot have anticipated the extraordinary success of a play he took a decade to finish and in the end allowed to be performed only after the entreaties of his friends.

Tragedies and indeed comedies on classical themes had long been common in Europe. Shakespeare's Roman plays famously depended on North's *Plutarch* published in 1579.

Julius Caesar was almost certainly written twenty years later, and *Antony and Cleopatra* and *Coriolanus*, both also largely based on Plutarch, followed in 1606 and 1608 respectively. Not all Roman dramas were inspired by Plutarch. Ben Jonson wrote a *Catiline* inspired by Sallust and a *Sejanus* based on Tacitus. The latter was a terrible flop, despite (or because of) its extreme learning. The comedies reworked Plautus and Terence. The greatest classical dramatists of seventeenth-century France, Corneille and Racine, both looked to Euripidean and Senecan drama as models. Corneille's *Cinna*, produced in 1640, dealt with the Augustan conspirator, and Racine's *Britannicus* of 1669 dealt with Nero's murder of his stepbrother. These plays shared a fascination with the politics of the court, and added new elements. The court in its turn was fascinated with the drama. The court of King James and the sinister circle of Richelieu were equally interested in what political themes appeared on the stage. Romantic sub-plots tangled with the political, and unrequited love and rivalry between suitors and brothers added new levels of motivation. These dramas staged conflicts between love and duty, between personal good and wider interests, between family and state, conflicts central to the cultural life of Reformation Europe. Rapidly moving romantic plots surrounded the central theme with a swirl of conflicts, misunderstandings and shifting alliances.

Addison's *Cato* drew on all these traditions. It had a Senecan epitaph, asking how Jupiter himself could wish for any more wonderful sight on earth than that of Cato, steadfast among the ruins of the commonwealth. The action respects the Unities established in classical drama. It takes place entirely in Utica and over the final day of Cato's life, and at its centre is Cato's dilemma over whether to live or die. News has already come of Caesar's victory at Thapsus. Waiting in the city for his arrival are a cast of senators, already beginning to waver in their loyalty to the Pompeian cause, along with their local Numidian allies. Entangled with the political drama there are dramatic threads too, the love that the Numidian prince Juba has for Cato's daughter Marcia, and the rivalry of Cato's two sons for the love of Lucia, daughter of one of the two senators. First performed in Drury Lane in 1713, Addison's *Cato* was an immediate success. There were more than two hundred stagings in eighteenth-century England alone, and more than twenty reprintings. Pope hailed it as restoring native British drama, which had subsisted too long 'on French translation, and Italian song'. The reception was if anything even more rapturous in the colonies. Following its first American performance in Charleston, South Carolina, in 1735, it was performed in all the metropolitan centres. Some touring companies performed only *Cato*, making it perhaps one of the most popular dramas in early America. Quotations from the play were ubiquitous in the political writings and speeches of the 1760s and 1770s. It was George Washington's favourite play, and was performed by his troops at Valley Forge in 1778. The citizens of Philadelphia came out to spectate.

Why Cato? The play reads oddly today. Modern critics complain about the blend of romantic and political plots, although that was conventional for the period and looks back to the plots of Corneille and Racine. There is little action, even for a classical drama. Cato appears at the beginning of Act II to give a resolute answer to Caesar's ambassador. The rest of the play consists of the bleeding away of support and the progress of various romantic intrigues. Cato kills himself at the beginning of Act V, ensuring with

19. Philip Kemble plays a nobler and more dignified Cato in Addison's play. This fine portrait is from the Garrick Club and commemorates what, along with the part of Coriolanus, was one of his favorite roles. An extract from Cato was read out at his funeral in 1823.

his dying words the resolution of the various romances in favour of the more loyal of his followers. The play has been described as a dialogue in poems, and as a series of high-minded speeches rather than a drama proper. Yet the failure of the text to grasp most modern imaginations highlights a difference in audience rather than a deficiency in the play. For American colonists, at least, it was the succession of bold assertions of the value of liberty and patriotism in the face of tyranny that impressed. For Republicans, the attraction was even more obvious in the face of George III's government. During the French Revolution, too, *Cato* struck a chord. Voltaire had proclaimed the play Addison's masterpiece and the finest tragedy written in English. Its ethical stance helped its appeal, as well as what it had taken from French classical drama. A *Caton d'Utique* was written during the Terror by François Raynoud, in prison at the time. Another play of the same name by Philippe Tardieu Saint-Michel was performed on the 20th Germinal of Year Four. It is a pale shadow of Addison's play, on which it is clearly based, but with all romance and exotic African setting stripped out, a set of speeches in clunky Alexandrines that cannot compare to Racine's verse. But it testifies to the power of the play, and of Cato Uticensis. More dramatically gripping are the three paintings of the death of Cato, all awarded the Grand Prix de Rome in 1797 when the competition was re-established following a break during the Revolution. By Bouchet, Bouillon and Guerin, they all faithfully follow Plutarch, with varying degree of anatomical grotesqueness. Cato offered a means of grafting revolutionary sentiment on to the classical tradition.

The popularity of *Cato* in England before the American and French revolutions is a more complex matter. Whigs and Tories both claimed it embodied their core values. It played to a contemporary taste for classical themes, and satisfied a morbid fascination with deathbed scenes and perhaps also a growing interest in exotic non-European characters, of whom Juba and his Numidians are representatives. More importantly it embodied a moral position that did not jar with Christian values, and which cohered with a patriotism already evolving into nationalism. It was (and remains) eminently quotable. So Cato rejects the offer of mercy brought by Caesar's envoy Decius with these words:

> My life is grafted on the fate of Rome
> Would he save Cato, bid him spare his country.
> Tell your dictator this; and tell him Cato
> Disdains a life which he has power to offer.

And in his last dying speech, he entrusts his daughter Marcia to the Numidian prince Juba.

> A senator of Rome, while Rome survived
> Would not have matched his daughter with a king –
> But Caesar's arms have thrown down all distinction –
> I'm sick to death – Oh when shall I get loose
> From this vain world, the abode of guilt and sorrow!
> And yet, methinks a beam of light breaks in
> On my departing soul – Alas I fear
> I've been too hasty! Oh ye powers that search
> The heart of man, and weigh his innermost thoughts,
> If I have done amiss, impute it no –
> The best may err, but you are good, and – Oh! (*Dies*.)

The decent senator Lucius closes the play by echoing the sentiment that Cato's death is the end of Rome. Notice how Addison deals, as all Christian admirers of Cato have had to, with the sin of suicide. His Cato seems to have beatific vision, and a chance to die repentant by Christian, if not by Roman, lights.

Cato appealed to all those who wanted citizens to hold governments and tyrannical monarchs to account. Seven

years after the play's first performance, the first of a series
of radical political articles appeared in the *London Journal*
over the pseudonym Cato. The authors, John Trenchard and
Thomas Gordon, combined a conventional Whig critique of
corruption in the government and in the court with a more
philosophical interest in liberty. Philosophically their ideas
can be traced back to Locke; politically they opposed not
monarchy itself, but certainly any sign that the monarchy was
trying to re-establish prerogatives ceded in the Revolutionary
settlement of 1688. Dislike of Roman Catholics and High
Anglicans alike, together with respect for natural rights, led
them to challenge authority. Not Republicans themselves, it
is easy to see why they appealed to those who were. The
letters eventually numbered 138 and were all published
between November 1720 and July 1723, reaching a very
wide readership in the educated classes. They began by pro-
testing ferociously about collusion between government and
companies in the South Sea Bubble scandal. Soon they bore
titles such as 'The Arts of misleading the People by Sounds',
and 'What measures are actually taken by wicked and desperate Ministers to ruin and enslave their Country', and
'Considerations on the destructive Spirit of arbitrary Power.
With the Blessings of Liberty, and our own Constitution.'
Printed collections of the letters began to circulate almost
immediately. There were sixteen printings up to 1724, and
they were highly popular in the American colonies. Many
colonists would have already associated Cato with radical
political thought before they even saw the Addison play.
From 1733 onwards the four-volume third edition bore the
title *Cato's Letters. Essays on Liberty, Civil and Religious, and
Other Important Subjects.* They were widely read before the
American Revolution, and known not only to the framers

of the constitution but also to their critics. A series of seven letters of Cato were published between 1787 and 1788 in the *New York Journal* by George Clinton, an opponent of federalism. Trenchard and Gordon's *Letters* were also the inspiration for what is perhaps the latest reverberation of Cato of Utica in the contemporary world. When in 1977 a libertarian think tank was set up to champion the free-market ideals associated with Milton Friedman and in general to defend the rights of individual citizens against government, it chose as its name 'The Cato Institute'. Now well established in Washington with an annual turnover of millions of dollars, a major publication programme, and a huge team of fellows, researchers and support staff, it is among the most influential policy centres on the planet.

We have followed Cato a long way from his own day, and it is easy to lose sight of the original, misanthropic and mostly frustrated Roman politico, saddled with a famous name but growing up at a time when the opportunities for political life in Rome were so often diminished by the power of military juntas. Cato lived on mostly because of the way he chose to die. The flurry of attention he received until Caesar's death ensured him his place in Plutarch, and once aboard the *Parallel Lives* his posterity was secured. Yet there were long Cato-less centuries to cross before he found fame again. During the Middle Ages, Cato normally meant his ancestor the censor, to whom some verse maxims were attributed. Nestling in his Plutarchian survival capsule, Cato had his *Nachleben*. The moment of glory came in the burst of literary and political action which presented him first in Addison's play, then in Trenchard and Gordon's pamphlets, and finally to a colonial population who already knew their Plutarch backwards and were eager for symbols of fierce resistance to tyranny, a resistance powered by philosophy and virtue.

The story of Cato has one more thing to reveal about the way the Roman past reverberates. At those times when Cato was most recognisable – most present, as it were, in the imagination – he appeared in the most ephemeral of media. Plays, journals, pamphlets, newspaper headlines and political speeches all made Cato vividly real in the eighteenth century. His burst of fame in the first century AD was rather similar. But what preserved Cato, in the long gaps between public enthusiasms, were texts. At first sight this looks like an example of what is often claimed to be the relationship between 'high' culture and 'popular' culture. The great tradition is preserved in the classics and kept alive in the education of the few: wider enthusiasms are fed by works of vulgarisation. But it was the widespread authority of Plutarch's *Lives* in translation that made Cato a suitable symbol, and he was deployed as such not by the guardians of culture so much as by oppositional groups, Whig pamphleteers in London and colonial rebels in early America. Cato always speaks to political power rather than for it.

⧗

Every history of reception is different. But any classical text that dealt with tyranny and tyrannicide, conspiracy and mercy, was likely to be snapped up by writers or artists from the Renaissance, or as a vehicle for considering this most vital of questions in courtly Europe. In the last chapter, I related Dio's version of the story in which Augustus discovered a conspiracy led by one of Pompey's grandsons, Cinna, but was persuaded by his wife Livia to spare him, and protect himself with generosity rather than fear. Dio's narrative and Livia's speeches in it are impressive set-pieces, but they had little if any afterlife compared to the shorter version of the same anecdote included in Seneca's *On Mercy*. That essay offered arguments in favour of reigning mercifully, mingled with praise of the young emperor Nero. Early in the treatise, Seneca presents an image of the mature Augustus as the mildest of princes, his sword always guided by the interests of the state. But, when he was your (i.e. Nero's) age, Seneca goes on, in his early twenties that is, he plunged daggers into the hearts of his friends.

This is a familiar retelling of the story of how the savage Octavian who had signed the proscriptions and fought the civil wars was transformed into the magnanimous statesman Augustus who guided the republic into pacific monarchy. Augustus himself played a major role in constructing this myth after the Actium campaign: the propaganda of the reign suddenly makes much less of Caesar the dictator, there was no public rejoicing over the death of Antony, the triumph was celebrated over Cleopatra alone and there was some limited rehabilitation for those who had picked the wrong side. The twenties BC were an anxious time, and perhaps Augustus escaped some of the plots mentioned in the last chapter by luck as much as design. But Romans were good at learning lessons, there were no calls for resignation, and gradually the time and monuments reconciled Romans to monarchy. All the same, some asked how deeply buried beneath the first emperor's peaceful concern with monuments and piety lurked the young Octavian who with Lepidus and Antony had signed all those death warrants and hunted down Brutus and Cassius at Philippi in the name of Mars the Avenger. Was there a moment when the emperor finally realised the killing had to stop?

Seneca sets the key transition when Augustus is forty. Cinna's plot is betrayed to him and Augustus orders a council of his friends to assemble the next morning to decide Cinna's fate. But the emperor spends a sleepless night tormented by the thought of yet more bloodshed. He agonises over whether it would be just to spare Cinna, after all the carnage of the civil wars, or whether it is right that his own survival should be the cause of yet more executions. Eventually Livia intervenes:

> Will you accept a woman's advice? Why not do as doctors do? When all the usual remedies fail, they try the opposite. So far you have made no headway with a policy of harshness. The execution of Salvidienus was followed that of Lepidus, Lepidus's death by Murena's, Murena's by Caepio's, Caepio's by Egnatius, and I say nothing about those others who dared to plot such a crime. Now make an experiment to see what results clemency will produce instead. Forgive Lucius Cinna. Now he has been caught he cannot do you any harm, but spared he will increase your reputation.

Augustus is delighted to hear advice he wishes to follow, cancels the orders for the council and shuts himself up alone with Cinna, to whom he speaks for two hours, allowing no interruption, before not only pardoning him but raising him to the consulship. The sequel was that Cinna became the most faithful of Augustus's friends, and there were no more plots against his life.

Seneca's philosophy had an enormous impact on the Latin

20. *This engraving depicts a statue once believed to show Seneca committing suicide by opening his veins in his bath. Although the original inspired Rubens, and was carried off by Napoleon for the Louvre, it is now thought to be a study of an aged fisherman. Collin's late seventeenth century image of it as a fountain spouting blood recalls the esteem Seneca was held in some periods, as well as a shift in our sense of the grotesque.*

church fathers of the fourth century. His natural philosophy was the basis for medieval science until texts of Aristotle began to arrive from the east. The twelfth-century scholar John of Salisbury admired him, and made explicit one source of his popularity that Seneca shared with Plutarch: Seneca's moral advice was highly compatible with Christian thought. Seneca's influence continued into the Renaissance. He was quoted by Dante, Chaucer and Petrarch. The first great edition of his works was produced in 1475, Erasmus produced his own in 1515 and Calvin's earliest work was a commentary on *On Mercy*, published in 1532. Seneca's tragedies were a major inspiration for the emerging theatrical traditions of every European country. The special attractions of *On Mercy* in an age of emerging absolutism are obvious. Medieval monarchies had often been weak, dependent on the support of tenants-in-chief, periodically threatened by the authority of the church and often critically short of funds. Not exactly constitutional monarchs, kings had been hemmed about by custom. As more and more powerful monarchies emerged at the end of the Middle Ages, the analogy with Roman emperors became more apposite. The title of emperor had spellbound kings since Charlemagne, but it was the emergence of powerful courts, of parliaments and of significant revenues, along with the limitation of the powers of great barons, that all over Europe created kings whose power could be thought of as above the law, like that of Hellenistic kings and Roman emperors. Renaissance scholarship and absolutist monarchy combined to make Roman politics 'good to think with', and Seneca's advice to princes was all the more relevant. No surprise, then, that Corneille's drama *Cinna* was first performed in 1642 at least in part to win back favour at the French court, and from its most powerful minister, Cardinal Richelieu.

Pierre Corneille was guided to Seneca's story by one of his greatest Renaissance admirers, Montaigne. His *Essays*, published in the 1580s, were immediately popular, being rapidly translated into other European languages and inspiring many imitations. Like the first vernacular translations of Plutarch's *Lives*, they formed a means by which classical culture was suddenly made available to a much wider audience. The anecdote of Cinna, in effect a slightly abbreviated translation of Seneca's account, appears in the twenty-third essay, which is precisely concerned with its contemporary relevance. Montaigne paired it with an anecdote about a similar act of clemency by a French prince of his own day. The stories introduced a meditation on the misery that princes live in if they allow the constant threat of assassination to obsess them. Like Dio, Seneca and all their Hellenistic predecessors, Montaigne was a creature of the court: he knew its political and ethical dilemmas and had his own interests in urging clemency on monarchs. If he was less optimistic about its efficacy than was Seneca, Corneille chose not to incorporate those doubts in his *Cinna*, which had the subtitle *The Clemency of Augustus*.

Corneille's drama is like Addison's in adding romantic plots to the political ones. Cinna remains the grandson of Pompey, but his motivations for plotting the assassination of Augustus are complex, as he has also sworn to do this as a token of his love for Emilie, the daughter of one of the proscribed. She too has doubts, expressed in her prologue. She is well aware the outcome of a plot is uncertain and that although Augustus's death will avenge her father, it may bring new disasters. And Augustus is charismatic. Like Addison's Cato he waits until the second act to appear and then dominates the stage. Even Emilie feels this. When we learn that courtiers beg her to intercede with them, so great is her influence with Augustus, and when she declares she would even take the place of the empress Livia if it would further her aims, it is clear that hate is not the only powerful motor. From the start Cinna is a reluctant conspirator, half-way persuaded that Augustus does not deserve to die, embarrassed by the faith Augustus puts in him.

Emilie's own confidante, Fulvie, presents her with a similar view. Augustus's rule seems better every day, as if he is making up for the sins of his youth. The honour and trust he shows at court to Emilie, Cinna and the co-conspirator Maxime is just one sign of this. So far Corneille travels with Seneca in portraying the ageing prince repenting of the excesses of his violent youth. But Corneille goes even further in the second act, when Cinna and Maxime are summoned to Augustus's presence. They, and perhaps the audience, assume all has been discovered.

But when Augustus does eject everyone else and have the two conspirators sit down, a twist is revealed. In a passage that owes something to Dio's debate between Agrippa and Maecenas – to which Augustus alludes – it turns out that he wants their advice on whether or not he should resign the throne! The power he wished for has turned out to be a poisoned chalice. He is surrounded by cares and fears. The precedents of Sulla and Caesar are evoked, and the injustice of their fates. Sulla, cruel and barbarous as he was, died in peace surrounded by his loved ones, like a good citizen in the heart of his own country. Caesar, although entirely gentle, was assassinated in the midst of the senate house. But precedents cannot always be trusted: the same course of action may lead to one man's death and the other's survival. Corneille makes the key connection here, that the clemency Augustus contemplates, like the assassination Emilie desires, may not have the same outcome as Caesar's mercy or his murder.

The drama unfolds through the tangling and untangling of plots. Cinna, realising that resignation would frustrate his oath to assassinate the 'tyrant', is compelled to argue that Augustus should stay in power. Maxime takes Agrippa's role as advocate of restoring the republic. Cinna's advice prevails and Augustus agrees to continue in power for

Rome's sake only. But the conspiracy fails because Cinna and Maxime are also rivals for Emilie's love. That rivalry leads to the revelation of the plot by Maxime's servant. Horrified, Augustus agonises, and Livia offers the advice she gives in Seneca, but in *Cinna* Augustus rejects it angrily. He does not relent until he discovers the scope of the conspiracy and especially the treachery of Emilie, whom he says he had treated as a daughter after Julia's disgrace, and of Maxime, who admits he betrayed the others out of jealousy for Emilie's love rather than loyalty to Augustus. The play ends with reconciliations, between Augustus and the conspirators, between Cinna and Maxime, and of course the romantic union of Emilie and Cinna.

Corneille's *Cinna* was a great success, not least with Richelieu. It is easy to see why. The reconciliation of honour with monarchy, the acknowledgement that tyranny can be disinterested and the wholly positive portrayal of Augustus were all comforting to a centralising monarchy with its own fierce critics. Conspiracy and tyrannicide were condemned. The reconciliation extends beyond those of the principal characters, since it puts an end to old enmities. Corneille signals again and again the roots of conflict in past wrongs: all the protagonists admit the catastrophes that preceded Augustus's reign. Like Aeschylus's *Eumenides*, this is a play about ending a cycle of revenge and feud. By the finale, Augustus no longer rules because he won by force the power he desired, but because Cinna has persuaded him that it is his patriotic duty to rule. His former enemies are recruited into partnership in the enterprise. Their common loyalty to Rome, combining with the essentially virtuous nature of each of them, effect a peace that is in the nation's interests as well as their own.

Corneille's *Cinna* is a masterpiece, and like Shakespeare's Roman plays, it emerges from a mass of similar productions. Conspiracy, revenge and revolution were popular themes. The events of the late republic offered many suitable scenarios. Corneille also produced plays based on the lives of Sertorius and Pompey. A mass of other tragedies were composed on Roman themes in mid-seventeenth-century France. The most important precursor for *Cinna* was the tragedy *The Death of Caesar*, written by Georges de Scudéry in 1635 and dedicated to Richelieu himself. Corneille alludes to the play in a few lines, just as his characters allude to Caesar's assassination and debate the moral worth of Brutus and Cassius. Roman history was not the only source of inspiration for classical drama, any more than it was for Shakespeare. Greek tragedy, the Orient and the Middle Ages provided alternative settings. Contemporary and biblical settings were excluded, but there was ample scope for originality. All the same, it is easy to see how the repeated issues of usurpation, regicide, conspiracy and divided loyalties drew on contemporary passions and staged contemporary dilemmas in ways that were overtly topical.

⧗

Cinna was propelled into the future by three chapters of Seneca and a few more of Dio. Cato of Utica owed his rich afterlife in the Age of Revolution to Plutarch's vivid account of his suicide. But the reappearance of the Ides of March as a cultural icon is a vast and complex story, one that is only now being pieced together. Shakespeare's play alone remains one of the most widely performed of his tragedies, in many languages and versions. But there were many other

Renaissance dramas, operas, films, even novels and cartoon strips, quite apart from a cluster of political ideologies – Caesarism, Caesaropapism, fascism, to name just three – in which the title Caesar has been given many new meanings.

It is easy to see the reason for the scope of his influence. First, Caesar has more than one claim to fame. Quite apart from the Ides of March, he was also to be celebrated for his generalship, for his key role in the creation of France and Germany, and of course for his connection with Cleopatra. Second, he survived in a clutch of classical texts, not just in a few mentions or even in one gripping account: his own writings, those of Cicero and Sallust, the biographies written by Plutarch and Suetonius, the histories surveyed in Chapter 1, Lucan's epic poem – and these are merely the major works. He does indeed bestride imperial literature – Greek as well as Latin – like a Colossus. Lastly, the rise of successive species of monarchy, from Augustus's Roman empire to that of Mussolini, made the figure of a man who established a dictatorship and was murdered for it a powerful symbol for both the supporters of charismatic rulers, and for their bitterest enemies. Yet the themes illuminated by the afterlife of famous Cato and obscure Cinna recur in the way Caesar's murder has been lovingly treasured, reinterpreted and, yes, staged and performed as the archetype of political murder. For we all know Caesar, and in a sense, if you can justify his assassination, no ruler's life is secure.

Compare Cato, whose life was eclipsed by his death almost at once. Historians, ancient and modern, remembered his part in the Roman politics of the sixties and fifties and in the civil war, but it was just the last twenty-four hours of his life that ensured his posterity. Dante remembered Cato's unorthodox marital arrangements, perhaps especially the scene in Lucan's epic when Marcia begged Cato to accept her back. When encountered on the threshold of Purgatory, Cato is alone again, separated for ever from Marcia as she remains in Limbo with other virtuous pagans. But when Virgil asks for passage for Dante in Marcia's name, and mentions her undying love for him, Cato responds that although Marcia pleased him so much when alive that he had done anything she asked, yet now that she resided beyond the evil stream she could move him no longer, as was ordained by the law made when he himself left. Beyond Dante, Cato's afterlife shrank again into the figure of the man who loved liberty more than life. This austerity of referents made Cato a powerful symbol, but a simple one. *Cato's Letters* could only be about liberty and tyranny.

Caesar, on the other hand, stood for so much more. His *bons mots* echo down the tradition too. Caesar's speed, his *celeritas*, made him a feared opponent. Who can forget 'I came, I saw, I conquered'? Caesar's clemency, resented in his lifetime because it made his tyranny all the more difficult to hate, incriminated his unforgiving murderers all the more. Caesar's supreme arrogance mingled in a strange way with his submission to destiny. He excused the invasion of Italy that began the civil war as an action that he owed to his *dignitas*, that is to his personal worth and moral standing. When Antony offered him a crown at the Lupercalia he refused it, saying, 'My name is not King but Caesar.' Impossible not to hear that as a boast rather than modesty. And when he cried that 'The die is cast' and he would accept whatever fate had in store, that speaks not of resignation but of confidence, a devil-may-care boldness. Caesar inspired his men to feats of heroism. No wonder after his death the greatest struggle was not an ideological one over freedom – that died at Philippi

– but a contest for recognition as Caesar's heir. Antony, in Alexandria with Cleopatra and the boy Caisarion, who she claimed was her child by Caesar, lined up against Octavian, now named Gaius Julius Caesar Octavianus. There was no single moment or slogan that summed up Caesar. Caesar was a far horizon rather than a point on a map, a style more than an action. Caesar offered no single model to imitate but rather a legion of referents. Later ages could choose their Caesar.

That process had begun already during the reign of the first emperor. Julius Caesar's adopted heir is conventionally known today as Octavian until the point where he took the title Augustus. But in his own day, court poets called him simply 'Caesar'. Julius Caesar was an ever-vital presence throughout his reign, but the form in which his ghost was invoked changed to suit the evolving nature of the new Roman monarchy. So Caesar the murdered father demanding to be avenged carried Octavian to the deaths of Brutus and Cassius. Caesar the general ensured the loyalty of his veterans to a young man with almost no military experience. Caesar the popular benefactor had started a number of great building schemes that Octavian could piously complete. After Actium, Caesar the dictator receded rapidly into the background, at least in official presentations. No surprises there, given that the priority after Actium was to avoid a repeat of the events that led from Caesar's own victory in civil war to his murder. Few of Caesar's titles survived unchanged to be taken up by his adopted son. Some of those honours had fuelled the conspiracy against him: all were treated as if contaminated.

Yet however unpopular Caesar's godlike honours *may* have been during his dictatorship, it was imperial cult of various kinds that did as much as anything to secure Augustus's position in the provinces and with the armies. The title Augustus itself had religious resonances, and in time he succeeded too to the position of Greatest Pontiff. It had been election to that priesthood in 63 BC which had first made Caesar prominent on the political landscape. But Augustus could take no chances. So Julius Caesar was condemned to impotent godhead. Eventually, as the Deified Julius, he joined Mars and Venus as one of the three divine ancestors of Augustus, all looking down from the temple of Avenging Mars at one end of the forum of Augustus, the great complex that neatly upstaged Julius Caesar's own forum while simultaneously proclaiming Augustus's piety in hunting down his father's killers.

Yet if Julius Caesar's importance as a source of Augustus's legitimacy diminished over time, he remained a potent figure in the Roman imagination. And it was his translation into a very wide range of texts that ensured his survival in a much more rounded form than Cato. The first of these texts were already composed before his death. Caesar built his fame in his own *Commentaries* on the war in Gaul and on the civil wars that followed. These artfully plain accounts of marches undertaken, battles fought and enemies defeated were once used to train schoolchildren in Latin. As a result they have for a long time been despised and treated as 'sub-literary'. But they repay careful reading. Naturally they enhanced Caesar's reputation and portrayed him as a brilliant and energetic general, ever mindful of Rome's interests and those of her allies. But they did more than that. Every great set piece account records – in the manner of a mention in dispatches – the heroic deeds of one or more members of his army. Sometimes these are young aristocrats, although that officer class also come in for their share of criticism. But most remarkable – and novel – are the many mentions of brave centurions and legionaries, plain citizens in other words, whose great deeds the popular leader records in the way ancient Roman historians had recorded the acts of nobles like Horatius, who held the bridge, or Coriolanus, who led the enemy army away from the city that had exiled him. All these features recur in the civil war *Commentaries* too, along with apologetics. Meanwhile the sparse third-person account of Caesar's deeds and thoughts offered the most austere of autobiographies. Speeches and pamphlets, now lost along with the notorious *Anti-Cato*, also put Caesar's own version into the public eye. Alongside these accounts, used by all later historians, may be read the many mentions of Caesar in Cicero's correspondence and his final speeches. And of course Caesar played a leading role in every Roman history, starting with Sallust, who eulogised him and Cato when neither were cold in the ground. Almost every poet writing under Augustus had something to say of Caesar.

Three texts were especially crucial in transmitting Caesar's fame. The first is the ancient biography by Plutarch which was carried from Byzantium to Europe and America by the same route as Cato. Plutarch's Caesar is a hero for all time, like his parallel Alexander. The second is another biography, this time by Suetonius, who set it at the head of his *Lives of the Caesars*. By the early second century more than one writer described Julius Caesar as the founder of the Roman empire. Suetonius's *Lives* became the model of Latin biography not only in late antiquity, but also in the Carolingian court. The third text was Lucan's *Pharsalia*, that epic written under Nero by Seneca's nephew, a poem that keeps its political cards close to its chest, but sings the tragic and bloody story of the end of the republic with Caesar as its assassin. Lucan's Caesar is both majestic and terrible, the nemesis of liberty and an impossible act for Nero, or any other emperor, to follow. His was the greatest classical epic after Homer and Virgil in the opinion of Dante, and of many others. Together these three texts gathered up into themselves the energy of their many precursors. Each of their Caesars emerges as a mass of contradictory impulses, but he is always animated by an enormous force of character. This was the Caesar that passed from antiquity to the Renaissance and beyond.

Caesar's afterlife exhibits even more clearly than that of Cato the interplay of literary and popular culture. As with Cato there are periods when Caesar was remembered only by the guardians of a few texts, and other periods when he enjoyed widespread recognition. But Caesar's stream never flowed as narrowly as Cato's. It was more like the Nile, a powerful force in all seasons, but occasionally flooding the entire landscape. Through the Middle Ages he was celebrated and admired, if only by a few. Brutus on the other hand was usually condemned. Those philosophers, among them John of Salisbury in the twelfth century and Thomas Aquinas in the thirteenth, who approached the Ides of March through Cicero's *On Duties* might be more sympathetic. But they tended to draw back either from actually sanctioning regicide or admitting that Caesar was unambiguously a tyrant. Others were more ferocious in their condemnation. Dante fixed Brutus and Cassius in the lowest circle of hell, hanging from two of the three mouths of the imprisoned angel Satan. The third mouth chewed on Judas Iscariot. Caesar himself is found among the virtuous pagans, even if he is implicitly condemned by the harsher punishment handed out in the Inferno to Curio, whose speech had encouraged him to march on Rome. That view of Brutus as traitor to his friend was the predominant one in medieval writings. In Italy, one index of how attitudes to regicide began to change is the attitude of successive commentators on the *Inferno*.

The Renaissance made Caesar, and his murder, better known. The popularity of Plutarch and the many dramas he inspired represented a modest flooding of the river. At the same time, a wider shift in thought about regicide made the tragedy of Caesar more than just the story of a great man betrayed by his best friend. The anonymous Huguenot treatise *Vindiciae contra tyrannos* (*A Defence of Liberty Against Tyrants*) was published around 1579, under the name 'Junius Brutus'. It argued that subjects of a monarch who acted against God were not bound to be loyal, and that killing an unjust king might be a virtuous act. This was much further than Aquinas had been prepared to go when he pointed out the unpredictable results of historical tyrannicides. For the author, Pompey, Cato and Cicero were good patriots in opposing Caesar in the civil war, and Brutus and Cassius were beyond reproach for killing Caesar before his tyrannical power was entrenched. Cinna's failed coup against Augustus, however, was condemned, because of Augustus's supposed legal sanction for his monarchy. With ideas like this, and the similar ones expressed by George Buchanan in his *On the Law of Kingship among the Scots*, published the same year, we enter a new era. Ten years later Henry III of France was murdered by a Dominican friar in an attempt to prevent a Protestant succession. Mary Stuart had been executed only two years before, to crush hopes of a Catholic one in England. Just a decade later, in 1599, Shakespeare's *Julius Caesar* was performed for the first time. It was the very end of the reign of childless Elizabeth, the succession was uncertain, rebellion was in the air. Shakespeare and many of his friends were familiar with the arguments of *Vindiciae* and similar treatises. Republicanism was beginning to speak its name. Fifty years after *Julius Caesar*'s debut, the English would stage a more sinister drama, the trial and execution of their king and the foundation of a Commonwealth, or in Latin a *res publica*.

The combination of a new willingness to think regicide, the vernacular Plutarchs, the popularity of drama across Europe as a form of mass entertainment and finally printing transformed the power of Caesar's murder to fascinate. Much of its power was offered by the twin possibilities of heroising Brutus and his victim: Plutarch above all others was responsible for this, and Shakespeare exploited the potential so brilliantly that critics immediately began to debate who was the tragic hero of the play. One early attempt to resolve the issue, that of John Sheffield, Duke of Buckingham, in 1722, involved dividing the play into two, to create a tragedy of Caesar followed by a tragedy of Brutus. More popular today is to read it as deliberately unresolved, whether for expediency in times dangerous for poets, or simply to offer a dramatic meditation on conflicting loyalties, to friend and country, and on the nobility and futility of regicide. *Macbeth* and *King Lear* approach similar themes, emphasising as Aquinas had the unpredictable consequences of usurpation. But Brutus, because of his unimpeachable motivation and the ghastly consequences of his action (responsibility for which Shakespeare, unlike Cicero, does not lay at his feet), offers the best possible arguments for and against the killing of a tyrant.

Other dramatic treatments took different lines. De Scudéry's *La mort de César* was produced in 1635, one of the models of Corneille's *Cinna*. The political tenor of this play is revealed by the dedication to Richelieu that begs the Cardinal to imitate the Great Dictator. Predictably, the tyrannicides enjoyed greater popularity during the French Revolution. Voltaire produced a *Brutus* (on the first Brutus who had founded the republic) and also *La mort de César* in 1793. His Brutus has already resolved on assassination after Caesar refuses to renounce his desire to become king, and even when he discovers that Caesar is in fact his father – an ancient rumour, but one that cannot but invoke *Star Wars* for the modern reader – he still prefers to commit parricide for the sake of liberty and his country. *La mort de César* was performed in the Theatre of Apollo in Rome with a spectacular piece of stage furniture, the great statue known as the Palazzo Spada Pompey, found in the Campo Marzio in the sixteenth century and believed by some to be the very statue at the base of which Caesar was killed. (It was not, of course, any more than one leg was really stained in perpetuity by Caesar's blood.)

Voltaire's play reworked Shakespeare in several respects, but perhaps the most important differences derived from the new political context. If, after the English Revolution, regicide could never again be treated as a matter of purely theoretical interest, after the French Revolution it threatened to become a fashion. The murder of Caesar was a popular theme in the great tableau that hung alongside repeated images of Cato's suicide in the *salon*. Yet these highly politicised treatments of the Ides of March in some ways diminished the power of the Ides of March to offer a space to think out the implications of political murder. Shakespeare's *Julius Caesar* offered consolation and doubt to kings and tyrannicides alike. Caesar and Brutus could both be pitied. Each could also be admired, indeed Antony eulogises both. Perhaps Rome is the real tragic protagonist, condemned to the awful choice between tyranny and tyrannicide. French Revolutionaries had no doubt that Brutus was a hero and his image was briefly ubiquitous. But Shakespeare's play, created in an age that could imagine the execution of a reigning king and the abolition of monarchy, but had not yet attempted it, offered many more opportunities for reflection.

The waters subsided to some extent after the great age of revolutions. Shakespeare's play remained popular, performed in London or America most years from the early eighteenth century. Oddly it did not enjoy the popularity of Addison's *Cato* in revolutionary New England. But it had supplanted Plutarch and Lucan and Suetonius as the main vehicle through which the Ides of March were remembered in at least the English-speaking world. Caesar himself enjoyed a new interest in continental Europe as a prototype for the leaders of national states. Napoleon I and Napoleon III wrote commentaries on Caesar's. The former was fascinated by the brilliant general who had made himself emperor. The revolutionaries' interest in Roman Republicanism offered Napoleon a script, and a clutch of symbols to which the Egyptian expedition contributed more. Napoleon III invested considerable resources in excavating and monumentalising the battlefields of Caesar's Gallic War. Fascination with the Gauls, known best through Caesar's account, grew in nineteenth-century France as the alternative ancestors, the Franks, were associated with the aristocracy overcome in the revolution and with France's German opponents. Interest in Roman France grew for similar reasons. The symbols laid down in this period have been taken up and redeployed repeatedly in French culture

RSC
GREEN ROOM BAR

'I'm in our new production of Julius Caesar.
It's set in Rome and we're all wearing togas'

*21. Scenes You Seldom See. Caesar is so often in modern dress, it sometimes
requires an effort to see the Renaissance Tragedy behind the images of
fascism and military juntas.*

ever since, up to and including the phenomenal popularity of Astérix. But it is Caesar the general, Caesar the conqueror of Gaul and Caesar the emperor who fascinate, not
murdered Caesar.

The next great flood was not until the 1930s. Here the lead
was given by European fascism, especially in Mussolini's
Italy. The story of Mussolini's early fascination with Julius
Caesar has often been told, and the classical roots of fascist
architecture, symbolism and ideology in Germany as well
as Italy are now better appreciated. As Mussolini's ambitions grew, the emperors and Augustus in particular came

to overshadow Caesar, and of course the Ides of March were hardly likely to be emphasised in fascist propaganda. Yet fascism did alter the ways others saw Caesar. Ronald Syme's 1939 masterpiece of ancient historical narrative, *The Roman Revolution*, in its treatment of the rise of Augustus as the insidious work of a faction powered above all by propagandists, showed the clear influence of the fascist movements of its day, even if this was not made explicit. Fascism also made staging Shakespeare's play once again a potentially political act. The play was controversial in Mussolini's Italy. Fascist symbolism and costumes were featured by Orson Welles in 1937 in a famous production at the Mercury Theater which employed the then revolutionary device of modern dress: in place of white togas the Romans wore black para-military costumes, instantly recognisable from newsreels, and delivered fascist salutes. This sort of imagery continued to recur in modern dress performances until Trevor Nunn's 1972 RSC production. Joseph Mankiewicz's 1953 Hollywood film of the play, starring James Mason, Marlon Brando and John Gielgud, certainly had resonance for post-war audiences. Some of the pageantry deliberately evoked Nazi ceremonial. More recently other tyrannies have provided modern dress. Latin America has been a popular setting, but the range of possible referents is enormous, and has been exploited to the full. It is so often performed in modern dress that a *Private Eye* cartoon recently presented a group of actors performing it in togas as a daring innovation.

Today, Caesar's afterlife spills out like the delta in every direction, different streams dividing and running back into each other as Caesar reappears in every conceivable medium. The romance of Cleopatra accounts for much of his current popularity. The only great operatic treatment of Caesar is

22. *Antony sings in Handel's opera, watched by a kneeling Cleopatra and a resplendent Caesar.*

Handel's *Giulio Cesare*, which was first performed in 1724 as part of his project of bringing Italian tastes to London. Caesar, sung by a castrato, is a youthful and dashing hero coming to the rescue of Cleopatra in Alexandria. More recent Cleopatras descend from Shakespeare's reworking of Plutarch's *Antony*. But the streams mingle and intersect. The 1963 movie with Burton and Taylor may have looked back to Shakespeare, but in the pastiches it inspired Julius Caesar returns to displace Antony. *Carry on Cleo,* produced in 1964, is most memorable not for the Queen of Egypt but for Kenneth Williams as Caesar screeching, 'Infamy! Infamy! They've all got it in for me!' Sid James's Mark Antony has become a grizzled suburban adulterer, half-heartedly plotting against his boss to conceal his affair with a Cleopatra who appropriately went on to a more celebrated role in

Coronation Street. The French comic-novel *Astérix et Cléopâtre* appeared in 1965, also inspired by the Burton/Taylor movie, but Antony is completely absent from it. Instead we have the patrician Caesar who plays a part in so many of the *Astérix* books, with the magnificent *hauteur* of a great French politician, often reduced to rage but always capable finally of the magnanimous gesture. The Cleopatra he woos has the temper of a Hollywood actress, but a very pretty nose. Caesar originally entered the *Astérix* novels as the commentator of the Gallic Wars, obsessively commenting in his actions in the third person, and frequently quoting his most famous Latin tags. Caesar's special place in French national identity is presumably one reason for the success of the series. But Astérix's Caesar is multi-dimensional. If he is often the conquering general, he is also often the remote presidential figure surrounded by toadying ministers and harassed by a senate ever on the watch for his mistakes. Yet the Ides of March demand their place and he is forever followed about by a sulky Brutus playing with his dagger.

Since Shakespeare, Caesar's murder hangs over most dramatic representations of his life. This is true of Shaw's play *Caesar and Cleopatra*, written in 1898 and performed in 1906. The relationship between the protagonists could not be more different than in Handel's opera. Caesar is first greeted by Cleopatra as 'Old gentleman' and has some of the world-weariness of Shakespeare's Caesar. Cleopatra is a savage child, beguiling, charming and genuinely vicious. Their 'romance' is in fact a mentoring process. The future belongs to Cleopatra, but without Caesar's wisdom it will be squandered in a cycle of feud and murder. Shaw can't resist pointing on (or back) to Shakespeare's *Antony and Cleopatra* too in Caesar's farewell speech.

23. *Asterix's Caesar is as magnanimous and grandiloquent as any president of the fifth republic, but he is forever followed around by a thuggish Brutus. But as the dramatic date never moves on – Caesar is forever dictator, in a Rome more splendid than that of any of his successors – Brutus' dagger never punctures more than Caesar's pomposity.*

> Come, Cleopatra: forgive me and bid me farewell; and I will send you a man, Roman from head to heel and Roman of the noblest; not old and ripe for the knife; not lean in the arms and cold in the heart; not hiding a bald head under his conqueror's laurels; not stooped with the weight of the world on his shoulders; but brisk and fresh, strong and young, hoping in the morning, fighting in the day, and revelling in the evening. Will you take such a one in exchange for Caesar?

The play speaks for and to a British empire self-consciously at the high-water mark of its influence (and occupying Egypt at the time of its composition). Caesar's imminent demise, frequently predicted in the dialogue, is as essential to its purpose as is Cleopatra's vigorous youth.

Shakespeare's play is now the main vehicle for the Ides of March. Where Plutarch in translation once brought ancient

Greece and Rome into the homes of those who could not send their children to schools that taught Latin and Greek, Shakespeare's *Julius Caesar* with all its spin-offs in popular culture now offers one of the most common routes into classical antiquity. Not of course in the UK, where Shakespeare's position in the curriculum and the canon has long been under siege. But across the breadth of what was once the British empire, it remains at the heart of a literary culture based on English classics rather than Latin and Greek ones. There have been distinguished translations. *Julius Caesar* was translated into Japanese as early as 1883. Julius Nyerere, premier of Tanzania from 1962 until 1985 and the effective ruler of his country for much longer, translated *Julius Caesar* into Ki-Swahili. A former teacher with a degree in history from Edinburgh and a man who adopted the Swahili word for teacher as his preferred title, he was surely not insensitive to contemporary resonances in an Africa in which every strong state depended on a single ruler.

Yet if Shakespeare's play depended only on its political resonances, it would have sunk as swiftly as the versions by de Scudéry and Voltaire. As a classic transported across the English-speaking world it has become available to all kinds of appropriation. Over one of the many dinners in Vikram Seth's *A Suitable Boy*, the gentle university lecturer Pran Kapoor tells some of his relatives how he and his students had put on *Julius Caesar* for Annual Day the previous year (1950) partly because 'the themes of violence, patriotism and a change of regime had given it a freshness in the present historical context that it would not otherwise have had'. A safe freshness of course. The women look on entranced, the student Malati because she has a crush on Pran, and his new wife Savita noticing that he does not notice the fact, and musing that it is the obtuseness of intelligent men that makes them so loveable. Pran's choice of *Julius Caesar* in newly independent India marks him as a force for stability in the novel, rather than a disruptive element, a conventional moderately anglophile protagonist whose radical streak is confined within local disputes over the curriculum. Arundhati Roy makes a different appropriation of the play in *The God of Small Things*. Rahel, returning to her childhood home in Kerala after years spent in Delhi, then Boston, New York and Washington, remembers her mother telling her and her twin brother the story of Julius Caesar and how he had been killed by his best friend Brutus in the senate. 'It just goes to show,' Ammu said, 'that you just can't trust anybody. Mother, father, brother, husband, bestfriend. Nobody.' But the twins turn Caesar's death scene, and his dying words, into a secret language, and use it as one more means of excluding outsiders from their private world. That secret world will engineer their downfall. Both novels show how, in modern fiction, the use of Shakespeare is a powerful means of characterisation. How you use the English classics shows how you are situated in relation to the colonial past and in the post-colonial present.

On the shifting sands at the mouth of the delta, the Ides of March flow in and out of popular culture of all kinds. Cartoons and comedies, historical movies and television documentaries, toga parties, science fiction and Roman detective stories draw on those events repeatedly, mostly but not entirely as viewed through Shakespearian spectacles. These aftershocks of Caesar's murder are now quite gentle, entertaining rather than disturbing in the main. But then the same might have been said of Cato during the long centuries in which he languished in Byzantine libraries and in a little-read Latin epic poem. Who can tell what posterity still awaits Caesar's murder?

AFTERWORD

Mark Antony buried Caesar and none of us any more have much interest in singing his praises. If imperial power is alive and well, the age of Caesars, Kaisers and Czars is – just – finished. Science fiction writers from Isaac Asimov to George Lucas have imagined future emperors in the stars. But there have been few beneath them for two or three generations. Kings too have largely lost their powers. Future regicides – if they cannot be prevented – will be attacks on peoples and nation-states by proxy, not on their rulers. Governments are too difficult to murder. Caligula is said to have wished the Roman people had one throat that he might cut. Perhaps some terrorists wish for something similar. But since Guy Fawkes, no one has even come close to killing an entire parliament. Even if the IRA mortar attack on the British cabinet in 1991 had succeeded, the business of ruling Britain would not have stopped.

Yet Caesar's legacy remains with us. Enshrined in Shakespeare's masterpiece – if nowhere else – he will be carried forward even into a future where the Caesars of Cicero and Plutarch, Shaw and Handel may be known to few. Maybe this is unduly pessimistic, given that he has Cleopatra to help him. Caesar's murder served to immortalise him more effectively than all those Roman temples vowed by his

24. Exit the conspirators …

would-be heirs. Different lessons have been drawn throughout history from his tragedy (and that of Brutus), but in most
the failure of political murder is apparent, as is the unpredict-
ability of its aftermath. Lop off one head and another grows:
the dominations of Antony, Augustus and all the rest show
the futility of Brutus and Cassius's plot, whether Brutus was
the noblest Roman, Cassius the last of the Romans or the two
of them the wickedest men after Judas Iscariot. Through the
long imperial centuries of Rome and Byzantium, the lesson
that murder at the court most often ushers in chaotic violence was taught, if not learned, repeatedly.

Like the Romans, our own governments personalise and
demonise some of their opponents. It is a seductive fantasy
that the world would come right if only the chess piece
called Mao, Castro, Reagan, al-Qaddafi, Saddam, Thatcher
or whoever might be removed from the board. History,

however, teaches the lesson that killing Caesar mostly fails. That is, of course, a pragmatic rather than an ethical argument against assassination. It is fascinating to observe how many great thinkers in the western tradition have devoted their energies to developing justifications for tyrannicide. Cicero was to be followed by Aquinas, who built on classical political theory to painstakingly set out the risks and proprieties of deposing a tyrant. Thomas Hobbes offered similar consolation in the English Revolution. It is easy to imagine the Utilitarian arguments for killing one man to free the multitude. But the limitations of those moralities are plain to see in the futility of Brutus's dagger, and the awesome power of Caesar's vast ghost.

FURTHER READING

GENERAL AND INTRODUCTORY

For a vivid and exciting account of the implosion of the Roman republic it is difficult to do better than Tom Holland's marvellous *Rubicon. The Triumph and the Tragedy of the Roman Republic* (London, 2003). Those in search of detailed coverage and background will start from the *Cambridge Ancient History*: Caesar is murdered at the end of volume IX but Brutus and Cassius survive into the first chapter of volume X of the 2nd edition.

On Caesar's career, Matthias Gelzer, *Caesar. Politician and Statesman* (Cambridge MA, 1968) is still the best guide, but Christian Meier's *Caesar* (London, 1995) is also good. Robert Garland's *Julius Caesar* (Bristol, 2003) is the most concise account of Caesar's life and significance. Perhaps the best access to Caesar the man is via his own writings. All are available in a number of good translations: the versions in Penguin Classics are vivid and faithful. The artful simplicity of Caesar's style, and the long use of his works as school texts, has concealed their extreme partiality and deft rhetorical purpose. The collection edited by Kathryn Welch and Anton Powell, *Julius Caesar as Artful Reporter: the War Commentaries as Political Instruments* (Swansea, 1998), gives some idea of how tricky he could be. So too does John Henderson's 'XPDNC:

writing Caesar (*On the Civil War*)', in his *Fighting for Rome. Poets and Caesars, History and Civil War* (Cambridge, 1998) and Llewelyn Morgan's '"Levi quidem de re ...": Julius Caesar as tyrant and pedant', *Journal of Roman Studies* 87 (1997).

CHAPTER 1: 'THEN FALL, CAESAR!'

Caesar's dictatorship is dealt with exhaustively by Zvi Yavetz, *Julius Caesar and His Public Image* (London, 1983). Ronald Syme's account in *The Roman Revolution* (Oxford, 1939) remains worth reading for its romantic interpretation of a Caesar who had reached the end of his ambition, and had little sense of what to do with his supremacy. Andrew Lintott's *Violence in Republican Rome* (Oxford, 1968) surveys the place of violence in Roman society and politics.

The events of the Ides of March themselves have been much debated. To Weinstock's comment and to the general works cited above add N. Horsfall, 'The Ides of March: some new problems', *Greece and Rome* 21 (1974). M. Parenti, *The Assassination of Julius Caesar. A People's History of Ancient Rome* (New York, 2003), offers a passionate and engagé polemic. Chris Pelling's 'Plutarch on Caesar's fall', in J. Mossman's *Plutarch and His Intellectual World* (Swansea, 1997), offers a subtle account of how the most important source dealt with the problems of multiple causation.

CHAPTER 2: TALKING TYRANNICIDE

The works of Cicero cited in the chapter are the best guides to immediate reactions to and thought about Caesar's murder. There are a number of excellent recent translations of and commentaries on Cicero's *On Duties*. A good introduction

is provided by Margaret Atkins and Miriam Griffin's anno-
tated translation (Cambridge, 1991).

Matthew Fox's *Roman Historical Myths. The Regal Period in
Augustan Literature* (Oxford, 1996) offers a subtle demolition
of the modern myth that all kingship was hateful in Rome.
The best introduction to Hellenistic thought on kingship is
provided by *The Cambridge History of Greek and Roman Political
Thought* (Cambridge, 2000), edited by Christopher Rowe and
Malcolm Scofield. The essays by Miriam Griffin, Christopher
Gill and David Hahm are especially useful. The best account
of *On the Good King According to Homer* is included in M.
Gigante's *Philodemus in Italy. The Books from Herculaneum*
(Ann Arbor, 1995). Elizabeth Rawson's essay 'Caesar's her-
itage: Hellenistic kings and their Roman Equals', *Journal of
Roman Studies* 65 (1975), is a marvellous exploration of two
models of leadership in collision.

On the Roman debates, *Caesar Against Liberty? Perspectives
on his Autocracy*, (Cambridge, 2003), edited by Francis Cairns
and Elaine Fantham, offers not only a splendid collection of papers but also two excellent bibliographies. Stefan
Weinstock's *Divus Iulius* (Oxford, 1971) remains the most
thoughtful exploration of Caesar's own thought and actions,
and Chaim Wirszubiski's *'Libertas' as a Political Idea at Rome
During the Late Republican and Early Principate* (Cambridge,
1950) helps understand Roman ideals before and after Caesar.
C. Sifakis's *Encyclopaedia of Assassinations*, revised edition
(New York, 2001), takes the story up the present day.

CHAPTER 3: CAESAR'S MURDERED HEIRS

The atmosphere and setting of the Roman imperial court
is brilliantly evoked by Fergus Millar's *The Emperor in the*

Roman World (London, 1977). An essay by Andrew Wallace-Hadrill in volume X of the *Cambridge Ancient History* provides a fine analysis of its workings.

But to get a sense of the atmosphere of rumour, fear, suspicion and intrigue it really is necessary to go back to the ancient sources, especially those written by insiders. Suetonius was an imperial secretary under Hadrian, until he fell from grace. His *Lives of the Caesars* are available in a fine World Classics translation by Catharine Edwards (Oxford, 2000). Andrew Wallace-Hadrill's *Suetonius. The Scholar and His Caesars* (London, 1982) reconstructs the intellectual and social milieu of his day. Cassius Dio, the Greek senator who survived Commodus and the Severan Civil War, offers a more detached view. His history of his own age is available in the Loeb Classical Library. The best study of it remains Fergus Millar's *A Study of Cassius Dio* (Oxford, 1964). The same scholar's 'Epictetus and the imperial court' in *The Journal of Roman Studies* 55 (1965) offers the view of an ultimate outsider, an ex-slave philosopher teaching in the provinces, but transmitted by the Greek senator who acted as his amanuensis.

The best global study of resistance to the emperors is Ramsay MacMullen's *Enemies of the Roman Order. Treason, Unrest and Alienation in the Empire* (Cambridge MA, 1967). A useful collection of essays is gathered by Adalberto Giovannini in *Opposition et résistance à l'empire d'Auguste à Trajan* (Geneva, 1986). The conspiracies of Augustus's long reign have been studied intensively. A good starting point is Kurt Raaflaub and L. J. Samons II's chapter, 'Opposition to Augustus', in Kurt Raaflaub and Mark Toher's edited collection, *Between Republic and Empire. Interpretations of Augustus and His Principate* (Berkeley, 1990). It was Fik Meijer who thought up the wonderful title *Emperors Don't Die in Bed* (London, 2004).

Some assassinations beg to be scrutinised. The best starting point for the assassination of Domitian is Brian Jones's *The Emperor Domitian* (London, 1992), together with his translation of and commentary on Suetonius's *Life* (London, 1996). Mary Beard's *The Roman Triumph* (Harvard, forthcoming) will include an exploration of one of the stranger manifestations of Domitian's attitude to the Roman aristocracy. Peter Wiseman provides a stylish version of Josephus's account of the murder of Caligula in *Death of an Emperor. Flavius Josephus Translated with an Introduction and Commentary* (Exeter, 1991).

CHAPTER 4: AFTERSHOCKS

This chapter would have been far better had it waited for the publication of Maria Wyke's forthcoming books on the reception of Julius Caesar in popular culture and also for that of Christopher Pelling's much anticipated volume on Plutarch's *Caesar*. The tantalising tasters that both have published have been enormously helpful.

How ancient Rome echoes down the ages is one of the fastest-growing areas of classical studies. Excellent introductions are offered by Catharine Edwards's *Roman Presences. Receptions of Rome in European Culture, 1789–1945* (Cambridge, 1999), and by *Imperial Projections. Ancient Rome in Modern Popular Culture* (Baltimore MA and London, 2001), edited by Sandra Joshel, Margaret Malamud and Donald McGuire.

The fascinating story of Cato's afterlife is told by R. J. Goar's *The Legend of Cato Uticensis from the First Century BC to the Fifth Century AD. With an Appendix on Dante and Cato*

(Brussels, 1987). R. Hamowy has produced a very helpful two-volume edition of the 'Letters of Cato' as J. Trenchard and T. Gordon, *Cato's Letters. Or Essays on Liberty, Civil and Religious, and Other Important Subjects Originally Published in the London Journal between 1720 and 1721* (Indianapolis, 1995). Bill Ziobro's fine website on classical America at http://www.holycross.edu/departments/classics/wziobro/ClassicalAntiquity/CA97SYLL.html is an inspiration. The subject is admirably documented by Meyer Reinhold in *Classica Americana. The Greek and Roman Heritage in the United States* (Detroit, 1984). Plutarch's post-classical career is told no better than by Donald Russell in the last chapters of his *Plutarch* (London, 1973). Among the many studies of Plutarch's approach to Caesar (and to Brutus, Cato and others) I would single out Christopher Pelling's 'Plutarch's Caesar: A Caesar for the Caesars?', found most easily in his collected essays *Plutarch and History. Eighteen Essays* (London, 2002), and Tim Duff's *Plutarch's Lives. Exploring Virtue and Vice* (Oxford, 1999).

Shakespeare's play has of course generated a huge bibliography. Apart from the usual commentaries, I found most useful for my purposes J. Ripley's performance history *Julius Caesar on Stage in England and America, 1599–1973* (Cambridge, 1980); Jack J. Jorgens's *Shakespeare on Film* (Bloomington, IN, 1977) for its fine comments on Joseph Mankiewicz's 1953 film; and Samuel Crowl's chapter 'A world elsewhere: the Roman plays on film and television', in *Shakespeare and the Moving Image* (Cambridge, 1994) edited by Antony Davies and Stanley Wells. On the background of contemporary debates about tyrannicide, Robert S. Miola, 'Julius Caesar and the tyrannicide debate', *Renaissance Quarterly* 38.2 (1985), and especially Andrew Hadfield's *Shakespeare and Renaissance Politics* (London, 2004). George Garnett's edition of *Vindiciae,*

Contra Tyrannos (Cambridge, 1994) makes thrilling reading for anyone interested in seeing how far the Renaissance mind could go in contemplating regicide. Corneille's *Cinna* is best studied in A. Niderst's *Pierre Corneille. Théâtre complet* (Rouen, 1984). Facsimiles of the plays by de Scudéry, Voltaire and others around the Revolution can be downloaded from the website of the Bibliothèque Nationale. Brutus's posthumous reputation is surveyed by M. L. Clarke, *The Noblest Roman. Marcus Brutus and His Reputation* (London, 1981).

Nineteenth-century political uses of Caesar have been surveyed by Peter Baehr in *Caesar and the Fading of the Roman World. A Study in Republicanism and Caesarism* (New Brunswick NJ, 1998). There is at least as much to say on the twentieth century. Highly recommended is Maria Wyke's 'Sawdust Caesar: Mussolini, Julius Caesar, and the drama of dictatorship', in *The Uses and Abuses of Antiquity* (Bern, 1999), edited by Wyke and Michael Biddiss, as an introduction to Caesar and modern tyranny. Tangential, but important, are the late Alex Scobie's *Hitler's State Architecture: the Impact of Classical Antiquity* (Philadelphia, 1990) and Luisa Quartemaine's '"Slouching towards Rome.' Mussolini's imperial vision', in Tim Cornell and Kathryn Lomas's *Urban Society in Roman Italy* (London, 1995). Other essays on this theme in *Roman Presences* and *The Uses and Abuses of Antiquity*. Happier memories are evoked by Nicholas Cull's '"Infamy, Infamy! They've all got it in for me': *Carry on Cleo* and the British Camp Comedies of Ancient Rome', in *Imperial Projections*. An introduction to the afterlife of Caesar in France is included in Tony King's essay 'Vercingetorix, Asterix and the Gauls: Gallic symbols in French politics and culture', in Richard Hingley's *Images of Rome. Perceptions of Ancient Rome in Europe and the United States in the Modern Age* (Portsmouth RI, 2001).

LIST OF ILLUSTRATIONS

1. Jean-Léon Gérôme's *Death of Caesar*, painted in 1859 (The Walters Art Museum, Baltimore)
2. Black onyx bust of Julius Caesar, from Egypt, *c*. 44 BC (Berlin, Staatlichen Museen, Antikensammlung)
3. Pompey, copy of a portrait of *c*. 50 BC (Ny Carlsberg Glyptotek, Copenhagen)
4. Aerial view of the Theatre of Pompey, central Rome (Museum of Classical Archaeology, Cambridge)
5. Statue long thought to be Pompey from his senate house. It is very likely a Renaissance pastiche made up of an ancient body and an ancient head (Palazzo Spada, Rome)
6. Reverse of denarius coin issued by Brutus to celebrate the murder of Julius Caesar
7. Tsar Alexander II lying in state after his assassination in 1881
8. *The Assassination of President McKinley*.Wash drawing by T. Dart Walker (Library of Congress)
9. *The assassination of Mr Perceval*, 1812, engraving from a contemporary pamphlet (private collection)
10. Plaster cast of a Roman marble copy of a fifth century sculptural group of Harmodius and Aristogeiton (Photo by Nigel Cassidy: Museum of Classical Archaeology, Cambridge)

11. Brutus by Michelangelo, 1540 (photo: Alinari; Bargello, Florence)
12. Portrait of Domitian (Museo del Palazzo dei Conservatori, Rome)
13. Detail of bronze equestrian statue of Domitian, changed into one of Nerva (Museo Archeologico dei Campi Flegrei, Castello di Baia)
14. Portrait of Caligula (Ny Carlsberg Glypotek, Copenhagen)
15. Portrait of Commodus (Vatican Museum, Rome)
16. Portrait of Elagabalus (Museo Capitolino, Rome)
17. Portrait of Maximinus Thrax (Museo Capitolino, Rome)
18. *The Death of Cato* by Giovanni Battista Langetti (photo: Alinari, Florence; Museo del Settecento Veneziano, Venice)
19. Philip Kemble as Cato. Painting by Thomas Lawrence, *c.* 1790 (photo: The Art Archive; Garrick Club)
20. J. van Sandrart: *Dying Seneca*, engraving by R. Collin: from *Sculpturae Veteris Admiranda*, 1680
21. Barry Fantoni cartoon reproduced by permission of *Private Eye* magazine
22. Eighteenth-century engraving of a scene from *Giulio Cesare*, 1724, by G. F. Handel. (Left to right: Antonio, Cleopatra and Caesar, played by Berenstat) (Lebrecht Music and Arts)
23. Caesar consults the auguries, from R. Goscinny and A. Uderzo, *Asterix and the Soothsayer* (London, 1975): © 2006 Les Editions Albert René/Goscinny-Uderzo.
24. Detail from Jean-Léon Gérôme's *Death of Caesar*, painted in 1859 (The Walters Art Museum, Baltimore)

ACKNOWLEDGEMENTS

I am grateful to Mary Beard and Peter Carson for their initial invitation to write this book and for their support and encouragement while it was in progress. Both commented heroically on earlier drafts. Thanks too to Penny Daniel, Annie Lee, Nicola Taplin and all at Profile Books for their help. Conversations with my St Andrews colleagues, especially with Jon Coulston, Emily Greenwood, Jon Hesk, Harry Hine and Christopher Smith, contributed more help than any of them probably realised at the time. The published work of Maria Wyke and Christopher Pelling has been an inspiration and an essential guide into what was for me a new field of research. Walter Scheidel confirmed my impression that Roman emperors typically reigned for less time than most monarchs and were more likely than any other kind of autocrat to meet a violent end.

Much of this book was written in the University Library of the University of St Andrews. Vital gaps have been filled by the Joint Library of the Institute of Classical Studies. A good deal of the preliminary thinking was done while I was an honorary research fellow at the British School at Rome, made welcome by Andrew Wallace-Hadrill and his colleagues. Wandering the sites of the city, including the tramstop beneath which Caesar was murdered, has made all the difference. I am grateful to the staff of all three institutions for their cheerful and efficient assistance, and conscious as never before of how fortunate I have been in my work places and in my colleagues.

The subject of this book makes this a wholly inappropriate gift for Jo Weeks, but it is hers all the same, with my love.

INDEX

PROFILES IN HISTORY

The *Profiles in History* series will explore iconic events and relationships in history. Each book will start from the historical moment: what happened? But each will focus too on the fascinating and often surprising afterlife of the story concerned.

Profiles in History is under the general editorship of Mary Beard.

Already available
David Horspool: *King Alfred: Burnt Cakes and Other Legends*
James Sharpe: *Remember, Remember: A Cultural History of Guy Fawkes Day*
Ian Patterson: *Guernica and Total War*
Claire Pettitt: *Dr. Livingstone, I Presume? Missionaries, Journalists, Explorers, and Empire*

Forthcoming:
Wilson: *The Death of Socrates*
Christopher Prendergast: *The Fourteenth of July*